JOURNEY BY CANDLELIGHT

Journey by Candlelight

A Memoir

by

Anne Kennaway

The Pentland Press Limited
Edinburgh · Cambridge · Durham · USA

© Anne Kennaway 1999

First published in 1999 by
The Pentland Press Ltd.
1 Hutton Close
South Church
Bishop Auckland
Durham

British Library Cataloguing in Publication Data.
A catalogue record for this book is available
from the British Library.

ISBN 1 85821 724 5

Typeset by George Wishart & Associates, Whitley Bay.
Printed and bound by Antony Rowe Ltd., Chippenham.

To the memory of
Mark John and Dorothy Kennaway

How many miles to Babylon?
Three score miles and ten.
Can I get there by candlelight?
Yes, and back again.
If your heels are nimble and light
You may get there by candlelight.

Babylon, it has been suggested, is a corruption of 'Babyland'. More probably it is the far-away luxurious city of early seventeenth century usage.

The Oxford Dictionary of Nursery Rhymes

Illustrations

Foreword

*I*n the sweep of a modern history book – whether it modishly analyses environment or conventionally recalls the flux of political events – the personal and everyday are quickly lost. So we ourselves become estranged from history. We seem to be remote products of it.

The value of a memoir like *Journey by Candlelight*, besides its intrinsic interest and charm, is that it restores a balance. In the recollections of a self-styled 'ordinary person' (the author describes herself as 'neither beautiful nor ugly, rather too fat, and ready for anything'), history becomes inhabitable and imaginable.

The trajectory of a young girl emerging out of sheltered adolescence here meets that of adult tragedy in the Second World War. After a childhood moving between Malaya and London, Anne Kennaway was among the last to evacuate Singapore before it fell to the Japanese, and was on the liner *Orcades* when it was torpedoed off Durban.

She is at once too life-loving and too sensitive to be 'ordinary'. In less honest hands her story would have been tinged with self-congratulation and the wisdom of hindsight. Instead its frankness lends it a poignant immediacy.

What, for instance, engages a young woman's eye and memory in 1940 as Europe is sliding into war? An oyster satin dress with diamanté hooks, and a blue chiffon hat.

What does she remember most vividly of the boarding-school she hated? No human face at all, it seems, but the cabbage roses on the wallpaper in the dormitory where she cried herself to sleep.

She describes the imminent fall of Singapore with moving and dramatic clarity. But it takes her by surprise, and even seems a little unreal: because she is young, blithely confident, and romantically in love.

This, you feel, is what it was like.

Colin Thubron

Introduction

I have never kept a diary. To recall those years more than half a century ago has been a journey into a tunnel with a lighted candle.

At first it was difficult to see much until my eyes became accustomed to the flickering light. There were times when sudden gusts caused the candle to burn brightly, and then the interior was very clear before the flame subsided and I continued on into the darkness.

Along this tunnel I have heard voices from the past and I have seen places I once knew and the people who were with me when I was young.

*C*hapter *O*ne

I remember that cold, wet day, early in March 1940, when I left London to return to Malaya. At that time I had not wanted to go.

As the boat train sped through the Kent countryside I gazed tearfully through rain-spattered windows at the sodden fields and leafless trees – and thought how hateful it was to be leaving Britain now that war had begun. So much would happen and I would not be there.

Crossing the Channel the sea was choppy. Wind and rain beat against the side of the boat. Fear of an enemy submarine increased my seasick feeling and Ma gave me a brandy to settle my stomach but that made it worse. I leant over the deck rail and heaved it up again into the surging water.

I was seventeen then.

War had been declared the previous September. So far there had been little action. Hitler's armies had not yet overrun Europe and the British Expeditionary Force was still in France. Food rationing had been announced and books with coupons issued. In London barrage balloons now floated above the city and some householders were building air raid shelters in their back gardens. Increasing numbers of men and women in uniform were seen in the streets, going here and there to new jobs and a new way of life. The winter had been severe with snow at Christmas and weeks of hard frost. Heavy overcoats, scarves tied round their heads, and inelegant winter boots were fashionable for women not wearing uniform.

During this period – later known as the 'phoney war' – the BBC had evacuated to Bristol and had not yet made those programmes which were so popular later on. Music and news bulletins filled many of the listening hours. Music hall comedians ridiculed Hitler as an enemy who would soon be overcome. Songs with the same morale-boosting message were constantly heard, one reminding us that 'There'll always be an England'.

Buttons (christened Mary Elizabeth but she had never lost her childhood name) was excited at the thought of leaving school a year early, but I had argued with Ma that I should stay in Britain. My friends had talked of the war work they were going to do. At eighteen I could enroll in any of the women's services, join the Land Army or become a VAD. Inspired by heroines of the 1914-1918 war, I saw myself driving ambulances over the battlefields of France or nursing in hospitals close behind the enemy line.

Instead, Ma was taking me away from it all – out to where life would be free from danger and excitement. Though not unsympathetic to my feelings – so loudly and passionately expressed – she had been firm. I was too young to be left behind on my own, she said, reminding me how much my father was looking forward to seeing us. She was sure I would like Malaya.

Snow was lying in the London streets when we went up to Marshall & Snelgrove to buy suitable clothes for the Malayan climate. It was strange to buy sleeveless cotton dresses, shorts and sandals when the stores were mostly stocked for winter and wartime. I had never had so many new clothes before. Ma said we would need them as one had to keep changing all day in the tropical heat. She bought us each four long evening dresses. I had a flowered linen one with a large white collar, a white lace, and a green taffeta with puff sleeves. The one I liked best was made of oyster satin with lots of material in the skirt, and the back was fastened with diamanté hooks and eyes. It was the most lovely dress I had ever seen. Long evening dresses were being sold at knockdown prices. There was little demand for them now.

Passages had been booked for us on a P&O boat, the SS *Narkunda*. It was still possible then to travel across France and Ma, never losing an opportunity to see Paris, had arranged – through Thomas Cook – for a two-day stay there before joining the ship at Marseilles.

It was raining in Paris when we arrived and it wasn't nearly as exciting as the previous year when I had been on a schoolgirl visit. My thoughts were of England and all I had left behind. The small hotel near the Madeleine where Ma always stayed was almost empty. People to whom she made conversation in her limited French were gloomy, apprehensive at the prospect of another war with Germany. The best part of the Paris stay was buying hats at a little milliner near the hotel. Ma bought one of the black tricornes she so often wore. Buttons had a straw hat with a large brim and wild flowers embroidered on it. My hat was made of blue and cyclamen chiffon with a swathe of the material hanging down the back. I felt it made me look sophisticated.

It was still raining when we boarded the night train for Marseilles.

Waking next morning and peering through the window of the sleeper, I saw a world bathed in warm yellow light. Months of sombre skies and wintry weather had not prepared me for the sudden change. It was my first experience of the Mediterranean. I saw a still blue sea sparkling in the morning sunshine, palm trees and oleander, houses washed pink and apricot with green shuttered windows, and gardens where tall dark cypress and yellow mimosa grew. The air was balmy. Bright colour everywhere was exhilarating.

That same afternoon Buttons and I were on the deck of the *Narkunda*, looking down at the busy quay. Baggage was being loaded; passengers and crew were going up and down the gangway. Voices shouting in different languages and the squawking of seabirds filled the air. I could see ships, big and small, from many countries, preparing to go round the world – the world where I, too, was soon to go.

Another phase of my life was beginning. Perhaps it wouldn't be so bad after all.

3

Anne and Buttons on the Narkunda, *1941.*

Probably it was the last voyage of the *Narkunda* to travel in the luxurious style of the P&O before she was converted to a troopship. Buttons and I took part in shipboard life with enthusiasm. We played energetic deck games, drank quantities of iced lemonade brought by attentive stewards and at meal times we ate our way through the long menus. After Suez the partial blackout was removed and coloured lights erected on the boat deck. There was dancing there in the evening and we could wear our new dresses.

The other passengers were civil servants, business men, planters, returning to India and the Far East after home leave. Some had their wives with them and there were other mothers bringing out their daughters. Young naval officers travelling to Hong Kong to join their submarine provided good dancing partners.

The voyage continued without incident. The ship called at the

Off the Narkunda, *Malta 1940. Anne, Buttons, fellow passenger, Mother.*

usual ports along the route and we went ashore, spending the afternoons shopping in Simon Artz store at Port Said, driving round in Malabar Hill in Bombay, having tea at the Gaulleface Hotel in Colombo, the way countless P&O passengers over the years had done before us. But for me it was new – I was seeing the world.

Ma had now relaxed and sat in the sunshine talking to old friends. They speculated on the progress of the war, on how long it would last and whether the Germans could break the Maginot Line. They did not think it likely that Japan would attack in the Far East – surely not, with the strength of Britain's forces there.

As Britain got further and further away it was difficult to remember the troubled world of Europe. We were an isolated community, day following day of pleasant idleness. An ocean breeze tempered the tropic sun. At night the firmament was ablaze with constellations I had never seen before.

Our journey lasted three weeks before we arrived one morning at Penang.

On the quay I could distinguish my father among the people waving. A small but unmistakable figure, his white long shorts were belted precariously low in characteristic fashion. Soon Buttons and I were flinging our arms around him. It was two years since he had seen us.

The car drove along the main road that ran north to south of the Malay peninsula through landscapes I had sometimes remembered. Under a brilliant blue sky were fertile plains of paddy fields and rubber estates, where sluggish brown rivers flowed, banked with lush vegetation. There were huge tin dredges in their self-made lakes, piles of effluvium like small mountains nearby, and there were villages of attap huts that clustered among trees. Never far away in the landscape was the jungle. Sometimes it bordered the roadside; it was always on the skyline.

Turning into the entrance of Escot Estate, the road continued through dark lines of rubber trees until it came to the clearing where the bungalow stood. And I saw again the home of my early childhood.

Chapter Two

My father, Mark John Kennaway, had been one of the first planters to grow rubber in the country. At nineteen he had left his home in a Hampshire rectory and had gone out to a tea plantation in Ceylon. The British Empire offered good prospects for adventurous young men. Three years later in 1902 he went over to Malaya, encouraged by reports that the rubber tree could be grown successfully in the western lowlands.

Malaya was not a British colony. It was made up of several states, each ruled by a sultan. With the sudden increase in trade, some sultans had asked for British advice and protection, and an agreement had recently been drawn up when Mark John first came to the country.

Enthusiastic, Mark John had gone back to Britain and had tried to get his conservative relations – and anyone else – to put money into buying some land. No one responded except his uncle's butler who had faith in him. Jones had known Mark John since he was a child and only he invested some of his savings in this rubber growing venture.

Soon after going back to Malaya Mark John acquired a small estate at Tanjong Malim on the Perak–Selangor border. Jungle was cut down to grow rubber, and among the newly planted trees a wooden shack, built up on stilts with a roof of palm thatch, was erected.

Named after his family house in Devon, Escot Estate was his home for nearly half a century.

The pioneer life suited him. From the beginning he was his own master, and his work gave him scope for his remarkable energy and inventive gifts. He was a small man with a zest for life, physically tough enough to enjoy the strenuous life, and able to survive the tropical diseases that were common then until remedies were discovered to alleviate them. He saw an encouraging future ahead.

By 1912 rubber sales were booming and Mark John was a wealthy young man, now richer than most of his relations. Jones, the butler, had also benefited from his investment though he continued to be in service with the Kennaway family until he retired. My father bought two more rubber estates, one nearby named Leonardo after his brother, and another in Perak at Slim River. An office in London was set up to deal with sales, managed by his brother Harold.

Mark John went on leave, travelling across America and indulging in his fondness for gambling – loving the excitement of a flutter. He played the casinos, placed bets on horses, bought tickets for sweepstakes and invested in unlikely shares on the Stock Exchange. He enjoyed it all – sometimes winning, sometimes losing. He was back at Escot when the First World War started and had tried to enlist, but bouts of malaria and dysentery had made him unfit for military service, and he did not go to Britain again until 1919. He was then a bachelor of thirty-nine.

My mother, Dorothy Hick, was eight years younger than Mark John. In 1919 she was starting her career in the theatre again after the war. Born in Yorkshire, into the family of a wine merchant who had inherited a long established business, she had grown up with her brothers and sisters in a small village near Leeds. They had lived in a large old house and enjoyed a happy-go-lucky childhood with little serious education except a series of governesses until their teens. The stables were always well-stocked as my grandfather had a passion for horses, and the children had ridden freely over the countryside. My mother was the only one of her family who disliked being on horseback. She preferred reading and was often found curled up in a chair or on a window seat with a book. When she was twelve years old she went to the theatre in Leeds and saw Forbes Robertson in a production of *Hamlet*. From then on she dreamed of going on the stage.

Life changed drastically for the family when my grandfather went bankrupt. He had neglected his business to buy yet more horses. Dorothy was then fifteen and at a boarding school, hoping to go eventually to Trees Academy of Dramatic Art. Now her penniless parents could not afford the fees, and she stayed in the school as a pupil teacher – an unhappy and ignominious position.

My mother, still determined to go on the stage, had gone every school holiday to London, and had knocked on many stage doors to persuade someone to include her in a production. During that time she met famous actor managers of the day who were sympathetic but not optimistic about her chances.

One day – after two years of perseverance – she was offered a small understudy part in a London theatre. It was enough for Ma to give up teaching for ever and consider herself an actress.

Edwardian theatres flourished. Whether it was music hall, melodrama, musicals or straight plays, they were a pastime for many people, rich and poor. Dorothy's ambitions leant towards straight drama – the works of Shaw, of Oscar Wilde, of Pinero, which were often performed then. But she took whatever was offered to her. She began to get walk-on parts in London theatres, she played at Stratford-on-Avon in the old Shakespeare Theatre, and she travelled round the country from town to town, a life of Sunday railway journeys and theatrical digs. After some years she joined the repertory company in Manchester run by Miss Horniman, whose leading players were Lewis Casson and Sybil Thorndike.

When she was in London she had a room at the Three Arts Club, started by Lena Ashwell for girls working in the performing arts. Young musicians, dancers and other aspiring actresses like herself stayed there, some of whom became famous. Dorothy made lifelong friends. It was home for her, she was a founder member of the club, and never gave up her membership until it closed down after the Second World War.

At the start of the 1914-18 war she was playing a lead part in a West End theatre. It was the end of her career. After that theatres began to close as actors left to join up. She left the stage and worked in a War Office department until the armistice. They were dark and sad years and she was too busy, she said, ever to go near a theatre.

A photograph taken of my mother at this time shows a shy looking girl, rather badly dressed, with large eyes and soft brown hair, and gives no indication of the drive and determination she must have possessed.

My parents first met on a wet November evening in London outside the front door of the home of a mutual friend. They had both been asked to dinner but the hostess had forgotten the day. Mark John and Dorothy had dinner on their own. Weeks later my father proposed marriage and, before he went back to Malaya a few days afterwards, my mother had agreed to share his life on Escot Estate.

After marrying my father she never went on the stage again. Telling her children – as she so often did – about her acting days, she spoke of them as a wonderful part of her life although she never seemed sorry they had ended.

Her first introduction to Malaya was the island of Penang where, in April 1920, her ship docked and Mark John was waiting on the quay. They married the following day. It was a simple ceremony at St George's Church with a few friends of Mark John there – a romantic setting this tropical island, surrounded by a tranquil sea, where palm trees fringed its sandy shores and where, among the old streets of Georgetown, different races mingled among the profusion of jacaranda, bougainvillaea and other exotic flowers.

After a honeymoon on Penang Hill when they were carried up in sedan chairs for no road had been built then, the bride and groom travelled two hundred miles southwards to start their married life in Tanjong Malim.

My mother found a sprawling wooden bungalow which, though it had expanded from the primitive house on stilts that Mark John had first built, had for over a decade been the home of a bachelor. My father had always been more concerned with the running of the estate than with his domestic surroundings. Extensive lawns now lay around the bungalow, but the interior was sparsely furnished with only basic necessities and little regard for comfort or elegance. Twenty seven half wild cats stalked the homestead – Mark John had not realised how they were multiplying. Servants had always looked after him. His meals were cooked over a wood fire in their quarters nearby, and a well-trodden path led there from the bungalow.

Soon after my mother came to Escot, Hi Ho started as the 'boy'. He was tall for a Chinese, over six foot, and came from a northern province of China. He stayed with Mark John until they were both old men.

After many years of London, life was totally different for Ma. At first the humid heat was very trying, leaving her exhausted until she became acclimatised to it. During the daytime there were lonely hours in the bungalow when Mark John worked out on the estate, and when she felt imprisoned by rubber trees. Nevertheless the first years were good ones.

In the early twenties many more people were coming from Britain. The European community at Tanjong Malim consisted mostly of planters. New rubber estates were opening up, and young men who had survived the horrors of the trenches came with hope to Malaya whose wealth was yet untapped. A manager of an estate often had two or three assistants.

The life of a rubber planter attracted extrovert types, sometimes misfits in another society, who liked an outdoor job and the freedom of colonial life. Visits to Kuala Lumpur, which was fifty miles away, were few, and some wives found their lives parochial, but most of them felt they had a better existence than in Britain.

Like other rural districts, this small European community made their own entertainments. Bungalows were without plumbing or electricity but everyone had servants in this prosperous time.

There were many bachelors and few unmarried girls. Social life centred round the Tanjong Malim Club – strictly for Europeans – where everybody gathered in the evening to play tennis until the light failed. Later the men congregated in the bar to discuss the endless topic of rubber while their wives gossiped and talked of life in Britain.

Women had recently bobbed their hair and shortened their skirts, and the Charleston and other new dances were all the rage. Entertaining was easy and parties of all kinds were frequent. Fancy dress parties, pyjama parties, any variety of party was thought frightfully amusing. Music came from anyone who played a piano or from records on a windup gramophone. Quantities of gin slings were drunk, often served from the washstand jug.

Rafting parties – an idea of Mark John's – were a popular feature of Escot entertainment. The River Bernam which ran though the estate was wide and shallow and, at a special place on the river bank, people got on small rafts, big enough for two, which been specially prepared for the day. Couples, manoeuvring them with poles gently downstream for three miles, fell off at times to the amusement of the others, and splashed in the cool water. At the end of the journey they met at the club to eat spicy curry washed down with cold beer.

Listening to my parents reminiscing, these were carefree days. Rubber paid good dividends and the sun shone in a cloudless sky.

Mark John and Dorothy were well-suited in spite of their different interests. Marrying rather late in life they were united by their affection for each other and their delight in their children. I was born in 1922 and Buttons came two years later. In 1927 Pippa was born and Susan followed in 1928. Four children were quite unusual in those days of small families – four daughters even more so.

During these years there were changes to Escot bungalow. It had become more imposing since my mother, arriving as a bride, first saw it. Visitors coming through the rubber trees followed a circular drive which, when it reached the steps to the verandah, was covered by a high-roofed porch, the other side of its arch leading to a covered enclosure where Mark John grew rare and interesting plants. The path to the servants' quarters was now cemented and protected by a covered way. A generator provided electricity for the household; kerosene lamps were no longer lit when evening came. With the family increasing, more rooms over more white pillars had been built when and where needed. The furnishings, too, were more luxurious and reflected my mother's taste.

In 1925 Mark John suffered a bad bout of dysentery from which he nearly died. Soon afterwards he won a large sum of money on a sweepstake. His six-month leave was now due, and my parents decided to spend it in Europe.

It was a year of great enjoyment for them. They skied at St Moritz, they dallied in Paris, going to all the revues and to the ballet where they saw Nijinsky dance. They gambled at casinos along the Riviera and for two months they lived in luxury in a hotel in Biarritz. Buttons and I and an English governess, who later came back to Malaya with us, went with them. Young and pretty, it was hoped that Miss Halstead might find a husband among the bachelors of Tanjong Malim.

My recollections of that time are shadowy. Dark red curtains in a Paris hotel bedroom, and digging in the sand at Biarritz are all I can remember.

The candlelight in this memory tunnel shows more clearly scenes of my childhood at Escot, playing with my sisters on the lawn, proud parents applauding every small achievement, and kind and gentle servants around us. I see myself riding my tricycle around the pillars of the bungalow, and remember the insistence on wearing my small size topee if I wanted to go out into the morning sunshine. No European went out in the day without a head covering. Some of the time Miss Halstead and I were closeted in the nursery where, with

Family and Miss Halstead in the new Austin 7, 1928.

instructions from the PNEU sent out by post from England, I learnt the alphabet and was soon able to read their recommended books – heavily abridged for children – *The Pilgrim's Progress* and *Tales of Greek Mythology*. I found them good stories and was glad I learnt to read at an early age. Many a child living in isolated parts of the British Empire was taught by this system.

In the hot afternoon everyone rested on their beds before bathing and changing for the evening social life.

One of my earliest memories is being shown the tracks of a tiger that had stalked as far as the casuarina hedge during the night. Silent and very frightened, I held tightly cn to my father's hand as we walked down to see the big paw marks on the earth between the rows of pineapples. For many nights afterwards I imagined he was by my cot waiting to pounce if I lifted the mosquito netting.

We children did not often go away from Tanjong Malim but there were special occasions when there was a big children's party at the

Selangor Club in Kuala Lumpur. Buttons and I, dressed in frilled organdie, travelled in the Model T Ford my father now possessed to Kuala Lumpur. The padang outside thronged with people – boys and girls in their party clothes and their parents – from all over the district of Selangor. It was a great excitement for us to see so many other children. All of them were under the age of seven. After this age the Malayan climate was considered unhealthy for their physical development, and they were sent to Britain, usually to boarding schools, seeing their fathers and sometimes their mothers too only at four year intervals until their education was finished.

My seventh birthday was celebrated at Escot. A few children and a great many adults came with presents, and there was tea on the lawn and a big birthday cake. The light fades quickly in the tropics, and when darkness came a huge bonfire was lit in my honour. The flames rose to a great height, eclipsing the fireflies which darted among the guests – as did we over-excited children until Amah put us to bed.

Perhaps, with the prospect of long separations later on, children in that society were especially cherished. In my early years I heard few cross words and much laughter.

Chapter Three

Some weeks after my birthday I left Malaya. With Ma and my sisters we sailed to England and soon after our arrival there, Buttons and I were put in a boarding school.

The school was in a country house in a village near Canterbury. My parents had chosen it for its reputation as a 'progressive' school where discipline was laxer than most of the schools of those days. Buttons, aged only five, was placed in the nursery section, but I, a sallow, sharp-faced child, found no protection from the bullying of my contemporaries. Bewildered at these new circumstances I became silent and withdrawn.

The people I encountered there are hardly recollected now, their faces long forgotten. But the house I remember clearly. Were it still to be unchanged today, I could find my way to every room in that creeper-covered building. I could walk up the long drive, a winter wind from the North Sea numbing my gloveless fingers, through a heavy wooden front door into the big hall. On the left was the large drawing room with brocaded sofas and armchairs, and long windows that looked on to the terrace and the formal garden below it. On Sunday evenings the whole school gathered here to sing hymns while 'Aunt Maud' the headmistress, grey hair piled up on her head in a very large bun, sat at the piano. I would stand near her, lustily out of tune, perhaps giving vent to my wordless woes.

I could walk up the wide curving staircase to the gallery that went round and know what was behind each door that opened on to it. The dormitories, Aunt Maud's bedroom, other staff bedrooms and the bathroom where two white iron baths on legs stood each side of the window. Nearby was a small room where the lavatory, a blue and white patterned bowl encased in a mahogany seat, was raised on a platform against the facing wall. Here was a refuge where I could sit in safety for a while until I was discovered. A passage led to the wing of the house where my dormitory was situated, and I would see again the six black iron bedsteads, and the large red cabbage roses on the wallpaper which I thought were so beautiful as I cried myself to sleep.

In this part of the house were the backstairs and, turning right at the bottom of them, the flagged stone passage led past the classrooms though I do not remember learning any lessons there. Another passage turning off it led to the back door, passing the junior dining room where the smell of fishcakes – my favourite – would tell me it was Friday. Beyond the big yard outside were the shrubberies – the area for secret games and where I was made aware of my inadequacies, never achieving popularity or even making a friend.

In the park which was surrounded by iron fencing, there were many old trees, one of them an enormous oak, reputedly planted in Norman times. On one of its main branches a swing had been fixed and, pushing myself higher and higher towards the sky, I so often longed to fly like Peter Pan – and leave the school forever.

My wish was granted. Within a year I went through the entrance gates for the last time – never to see the place again.

The Wall Street Crash in October 1929 brought ruin to many people all over the world. The stock markets plummeted and a severe recession followed. Escot fortunes drastically diminished and the following years were not easy for Mark John and Dorothy.

Boarding school was now impossible. To give their children the English education they considered so necessary, my parents decided that that they must live apart. Ma would make a home in London from where we could all go to day schools and Mark John would live alone in Escot bungalow and keep the three estates going. Many other planters had lost their jobs and for those that were left, times were hard. Trying to make more money to support his family he started writing articles on rubber planting which were published in the Malayan newspapers and read by planting communities all over the Ear East. The carefree days of the last decade had gone.

Thus I grew up in London. Our first home was near the Shepherds Bush end of Holland Park Avenue. Close by the traffic coursed up and down the hill, red buses going westwards through Shepherds Bush and beyond, others going eastwards up to Notting Hill Gate and the heart of the city. Away from this main road the streets were quiet. There were few cars and some tradesmen still used horse-drawn carts – sometimes an organ grinder played his evocative music on the corner outside our house. The houses, stuccoed cream, soon darkened in the polluted air – solid fuel was used in every home sending smoke up the high chimneys. Northwards the houses suddenly became working class streets which stretched for several miles. On the other side of Holland Park Avenue the houses were very large and wide roads led to fashionable Kensington. Holland House was still a private residence and the nearest public park was Kensington Gardens.

Darnley Road led out of Royal Crescent – a short street of ten tall narrow houses. Stone steps led up to their front doors and iron railings guarded their basements. There was a big bay window on each of the four floors. Number Five was on the corner and ours was the upper maisonette.

Inside the front door, one of two inner doors opened on to steep brown linoleum stairs. The first floor at the top of them had our drawing room, our dining room, a box room and the small narrow kitchen. Another flight of steep linoleum stairs led to a similar layout: a big bedroom, a smaller one, the bathroom and another box room.

Seven of us lived here – my mother, her four girls, Nannie and Mrs Nolan, our cook.

The furniture was ugly and cheap, bought from Oetzmans in the Tottenham Court Road. The drawing room – far less formal than its name sounded – was also where we children played. It was the only room not covered in brown linoleum – here there was a carpet and the wooden surrounds were polished. Two armchairs and a sofa upholstered in dark blue material with a coarse gold thread woven into it, were improved by pale blue velvet cushions made by Ma. A wireless set – in a large box with a fretwork decoration – stood on a table and in a corner was the dolls house and most of our dolls which, as a family of little girls, played an important part in our lives. In winter a coal fire burned all day behind a high brass fireguard; a large clothes horse hung with newly ironed washing often stood nearby. It was a pleasant room with the big bay window and high ceiling. The framed posters on the walls, bought by Ma from railway companies, were in clear bright colours and pictured scenes of seaside resorts where the sun was always shining.

The dining room, which looked on to strips of sooty gardens and the backs of the Norland Road houses, was strictly functional. Straight backed chairs with brown rexine seats, a round table covered with American oilcloth, and the sideboard – a small flimsily built piece of furniture with one of the doors never shutting properly – were the only furniture.

In this cramped home we all lived closely together. Nannie with Pippa and Susan had the top front bedroom, Mrs Nolan slept in the boxroom beside it. Buttons and I had the back bedroom beside the bathroom where a big geyser heated the water. At the lighting of a match a forest of little flames roared up inside and hot water slowly thundered from its spout into the bath.

Ma, sleeping in the other boxroom, managed on a very tight budget, endeavouring to bring us up as a middle class family. The house was run entirely for us children.

Though an exceedingly plain cook, Mrs Nolan, comfortably rotund with bright red cheeks, was very good natured, never objecting to Buttons and me being around her as she worked in the little kitchen. She came from Sheffield and was supporting her husband there who was unable to get work in those cruel times of unemployment.

This was Nannie's first post – a forceful young woman, fortunately with a sense of humour. Although only engaged to care for Pippa and Susan, she contributed much to this rather chaotic household, for Ma was no disciplinarian except for her insistence on good manners. Nannie became a family friend until she died twenty years later.

In this home I was a happy little girl, secure with my family again. The unhappy year at boarding school faded. The new school was only two streets away from Darnley Road – three high terraced houses, everywhere painted dark green and cream, and where there were a great many staircases and passages. Lessons were taught by dedicated teachers, each making their subject so absorbing. I thrived here and remember these grey-haired ladies, usually wearing dark suited coats and skirts, with affection.

How I longed for a garden where I could go out and play. The strip of grass at the back of Number Five belonged to the lower maisonette and was mostly used by Rex, the Alsatian who lived there with his owner Mrs Jones and her two daughters, both dancers on the music halls. To play in a green space meant a long walk, supervised by Nannie, up Notting Hill and through the gate into Kensington Gardens. As I grew older, though, I was allowed out by myself and could roam the neighbourhood. Soon I knew all the streets and remember my envy of those people who lived in houses that had a big communal garden in front, surrounded by railings and a locked gate where only the residents had the key. A street away from our house was Norland Market where I could push my way among the people and look at the wares on the different stalls – fruit and vegetables laid out, the cheap china ornaments stall, another with bales of cloth and remnants of material. Ma did her shopping here and bought quantities of mince from the butcher who also sold eel pies. Further away was Shepherds Bush Green and Woolworths where I could spend my weekly threepence on a bag of broken toffee pieces covered in chocolate. My cheeks bulging, it was a short saunter home.

Ma had a restricted life. She did not entertain and saw few friends except old cronies from the Three Arts Club. Her energies were entirely concentrated on bringing up her daughters. With her great interest in the Arts and the advantages of living in London she tried to encourage our knowledge of them. Buttons and I were taken to museums, to art galleries, to concerts and to places of historical interest. How much we absorbed as we scampered up and down the empty galleries or played hide and seek among the glass cases it is difficult to say. Afterwards we sometimes had tea at Lyon's Corner House which was iced cakes at marble topped tables served by 'Nippies' in their black dresses with white frilled accessories and where a four-piece band played light music and hits from current shows. That for us was the exciting part of the afternoon.

Whenever possible we were taken to the theatre. There were many children's plays performed in London at Christmas time; *Peter Pan* and *Where the Rainbow Ends* were yearly favourites and there was always a pantomime. If suitable for children – usually a light drawing room comedy so popular in the Thirties – and one of Ma's friends was in the cast, Ma took us round to her dressing room after a matinee and we sat impatiently among the discarded costumes and grease paint while Ma heard the latest stage gossip. Now and then we went to ballet at Sadlers Wells Theatre where the tickets were comparatively cheap.

On winter evenings she read aloud to us which she did extremely well. Buying second hand books for as little as 2*d.* or 3*d.* from Foyles in the Charing Cross Road, she collected a big library. Abridged of the stodgy bits, many a classical novel came to life when read in her expressive voice.

Every week Ma wrote to Mark John, enclosing our childish letters, and every week came a letter in his sprawling handwriting with news of Malaya. She hated living apart from him and longed to go back to Escot, often talking about life there.

The world slump had gone on much longer than my parents had anticipated, but by 1934 it was easing and the rubber market improving. Mark John came on leave again, having missed much of his family's childhood. In his suitcases were Japanese dolls and boxes of Turkish Delight. Though Pippa and Susan had been babies when he last saw them, they did not find he was a stranger. The following months were crammed with treats until he left on a P&O ship, leaving my mother to bring us up alone once more.

That year we had moved to a house two streets away – part of a one time vicarage – of Victorian Gothic architecture, where there was more space for us all. In the drawing room the ugly chairs and sofa were now covered in flowered chintz, and the piano for music lessons stood in the corner; its back covered in blue watered silk faced the room. We had a nursery in the basement but as we no longer played much with toys, it was more of a place to do homework. Around the walls were all the books that Ma had amassed over the years, and there was enough room for the *Encyclopaedia Britannica* bought from a door to door salesman and paid for by instalments over a long period.

Growing up here we were able to expand in our different ways. Susan, still a little girl, was already stage struck and determined to go on the stage – an ambition from which, like Ma, she never wavered. Soon after moving house I started at St Paul's Girls' School in Hammersmith. My school life there was also happy. I cheerfully walked there each day through the back streets of West Kensington, wearing a gym tunic, brown lisle stockings and my battered school hat, and carrying an attaché case full of books and skimped homework. My best subject was history, no doubt engendered by Ma's enthusiasm but, unlike Pippa who went afterwards, I showed no academic distinction. There was a great pride in the British Empire then and, with my family connections, I was especially proud to be part of it.

Mark John came back again in 1938 for another six months leave. As before it was a wonderful time for us all but I was aware then of the gathering war clouds. The following year, after my final term at St

Paul's, Britain was at war with Germany. Plans for my further education in Europe had to be abandoned and Pippa and Susan were evacuated with the school to Buckinghamshire. This was the time, my parents felt, to take Buttons and me to Malaya.

So once again I was at Escot Estate, a grown up now, neither beautiful nor ugly, rather too fat, and ready for anything.

Chapter Four

After our London homes, Escot bungalow seemed huge. Set in the wide expanse of garden, the harsh green lawns stretched out to the rubber trees, here and there broken by shrubs and trees. Bougainvillaea, hibiscus and other bushes made strong patches of colour, orange, scarlet, purple and crimson – as well as two large flower beds planted with red and yellow cannas. Another side of the garden ended with a high hedge of cazuarina behind which was the kitchen garden and a glimpse of jungle-covered hills.

The house spread out to the lawns in all directions. Supported on white pillars, the upper floor had a long verandah on two sides, shaded by green striped blinds. Wooden roof tops of different sizes could be seen above. At ground level the cemented area was mostly open to the garden but there were two sunken rooms. One was a formal dining room with large bay windows that looked on to the lawn, and with a red tiled floor. A great deal of polished silver was laid out on the sideboard. Electric fans in the ceiling had replaced the old punkah which still hung above the large dining table, its rope passing through to the other side of the wall where once a servant had sat, pulling it to and fro to keep the diners cool. The other sunken room looked on to rubber trees and had been the nursery where I had learnt to read.

Wide and shallow steps, flanked by pots of ferns, led up to the verandah. This enormous room had originally been the entire living quarters in my father's pioneer days. It was now furnished with rattan chairs, two wooden divans made by local craftsmen, covered with hard mattresses and scattered with gaudy cushions, and several small

Escot bungalow, 1940.

tables of carved Indian teak. Benares brass, Chinese porcelain, ashtrays, bric-a-brac and rarer objêts d'art dotted the surfaces. Above, in the high roof, little lizards – known as chee chows – slid around the rafters.

My father's 'desk' was at the far end of the room. This was a trestle table piled high with papers and on which photographs of his family faced him as he wrote. The revolving bookcase nearby held poor reading matter – only faded yellow novels, mostly Tauchnitz editions, with pages eaten by insects, and an assortment of planting manuals.

The most used area was the recess above the dining room window. Here were cushioned seats and more chairs grouped round a large coffee table with a decorated brass top.

Reproduction portraits of Renaissance beauties hung on the two long walls. Their formal elegance contrasted successfully with this haphazard room.

Swing doors led through to the bedrooms which were spacious

Front steps up to the verandah.

with long low glassless windows. Each bed was heavily draped with white clouds of mosquito netting. Leading out of each bedroom were the bathrooms – dark and cool with stone floors that had a soakaway in the middle and empty except for a large jar of cold water in the corner for splashing away the soapsuds after hot water, brought in by a servant through an outer door, had been used.

Everywhere was as open as possible, keeping the bungalow cool in the airless heat.

The staff were there to greet us. Hi Ho was now married with a plump wife and five sons, almond eyed and of varying heights. There was Cookie and Amah who were also Chinese, a Javanese gardener and a Malay syce (chauffeur) who wore traditional costume – a sarong of blended colours, white badjhu and dark brown velvet fez. The man who emptied the slops and did other menial duties was a low-caste Indian.

As I rushed round looking at everything, I thought of how in

Dining room at Escot.

England I had sometimes tried to remember Escot. I saw it now as our real home, unlike any other, that had expanded over the years as each member of the family had in some way contributed to its development.

Living on a rubber estate was full of delights before the novelty wore off.

The day began at six o'clock when the air was cool and birds sang in the garden where we sat drinking tea. Then my father drove through the rubber trees to the 'lines' a mile or so away from the bungalow. Here the Tamil labour force lived with their families in rows of huts. Here also were the smoke houses where the sticky latex bled from the tree trunks was processed into sheets of coarse brown rubber to be shipped overseas. There was also a little office where Mark John and his clerk worked till breakfast time.

During the morning which became increasingly hot, Buttons and I often bathed in the river or played tennis on the rough grass court in a far corner of the garden. Other mornings were spent in the bungalow, dressmaking inexpertly with paper patterns and cheap materials brought from the village store.

Sometimes we went with our father on his morning rounds. The Tamils seemed a highly excitable lot as they worked, hoeing the ochre yellow soil or clearing new areas to plant young rubber trees. They wore brightly coloured garments wound round them and their gums were stained orange with chewing betel nut. The foreman, Mr Asar Singh, was a Sikh, impressive in his turban, travelling round the estate on an outsize motor cycle.

The rubber trees were planted evenly in endless rows and little vegetation was allowed to grow underneath them. At the boundaries of the estate the jungle was dense. Tree trunks rose straight and immensely tall to a height of more than 150 feet out of the thick undergrowth of smaller trees, giant ferns and foliage. From the high boughs hung with creepers, monkeys swung; their noisy chattering could be heard above the sound of birds and insects.

On the mornings Mark John went to Slim River Estate, Buttons and I liked to go with him as there was a jungle pool there where we could bathe. We tracked along a narrow path, pushing aside huge leaves that barred our way. Sweat poured off us and insects attached themselves to our bare limbs. But at the end of the trail was a waterfall – a secret place hidden in the dark jungle. The water cascaded down to the pool below, glistening as the sunlight penetrated the trees. It was bliss to dive into its cool depths.

Mark John was always fascinated by the jungle, aware of the tremendous wealth that lay within this evergreen forest, if only he was rich enough to explore its potential. He was a keen experimental grower. Behind the casuarina hedge the kitchen garden had a large area of fruit and vegetables, and also his past attempts at discovering what the soil would yield. He had been the first person to grow tea on the plains of Malaya and had been quite successful at one time, though efforts at coffee and cocoa had not produced much result.

Buttons and I saw Escot as a patriarchal kingdom. Mark John determined the welfare of everyone there. He provided homes for his labourers, was responsible for their health, and there was a school for their children. He adjudicated in family quarrels, rescued Cookie from his gambling debts, and was the final arbitrator in any disagreement. He was trusted absolutely and his word was law.

We were happy to be with our father again – so indulgent and so young in spirit – and we laughed at his eccentricities. He had a great zest for life and a natural desire that others should enjoy it too. Every morning he rose at 4 a.m. and sat at his desk till dawn, writing copious letters and the weekly articles on rubber planting for the *Straits Times*. After a day on the estate he was never too tired for the evening social life. Unconventional and unselfconscious, he was known all over the country by his two names, Mark John, and was a well-known character.

My mother had a placid acceptance of his unpredictable ways. Over the years she had grown stout and her hair had become snow white but her wide blue eyes and her unlined skin gave her a youthful look. She liked to reminisce about her stage days and, if telling anecdotes, her voice was dramatic with theatrical hand movements. Mark John was proud of her theatrical past and liked reminding her of it.

The occasion of his sixtieth birthday came soon after our arrival at Escot. This was celebrated by a big dinner party at the Selangor Club in Kuala Lumpur. Seated among the guests and listening to the many speeches of congratulation from those who had known him over the past forty years, my father responded, looking across at my mother and saying that the last twenty years of his life had been by far the happiest. I – resplendent in the white lace dress from Marshall and Snelgrove – felt glad to be his daughter.

Meals at Escot were very simple. We ate chicken, rice, small fish from the rivers, and eggs from the diminutive hens that scratched under the banana trees. Imported meat from the Cold Storage was expensive. The fruits were delicious – prickly red rambutans with a small sweet fruit inside, papayas, tiny tasty bananas and pomeloes which were sweeter than grapefruit. Mangosteens were my favourite, the size and shape of a tangerine with a hard purple skin that peeled away leaving edible white segments. I never tasted a durian – the smell was too strong – but this large fleshy fruit had the reputation for being an aphrodisiac. Many of these fruits are now sold in supermarkets all over the world but in those days they were not exported from Malaya and were new to me.

Most of the meals were made by Cookie over a wood fire in the kitchen at the 'back'. In England Ma had recently learned to cook but at Escot she did not go near the servants' quarters. My father had a little kitchen made for her where she often made cakes, something Cookie could not manage.

Although she ordered the meals it was Hi Ho who ran the household, having looked after Mark John all those years Ma had been in England. It was Hi Ho who engaged the other servants; only he could work the generator. He was always there. At any time we called he would appear from the back stairs, ready to bring us 'ayah limahs' (the juice of fresh limes in iced water) or switch on the electricity so that we could play the radiogram. All his five sons had been born at Escot, they played in the garden at the 'back' and the elder ones went to school in Tanjong Malim. Three of them went down the drive every day with their satchels, spotless white gymshoes, blue shorts and singlets.

By midday the heat was intense. After lunch everybody went to their bedrooms and slept all afternoon. Later tea was laid out on the lawn with the silver teaset, cakes and fruit. A small burner using methylated spirit kept the water hot under the silver urn. There was no fresh dairy produce. The tea was a brown syrupy liquid made with condensed milk. In later life when I occasionally drank tea like this, I was always reminded of Escot at this hour. Against a backdrop of dark green rubber I saw us all sitting round the tea table in our cotton dressing gowns, our faces damp with perspiration.

Often there were guests staying, friends of my parents or some official visiting Mark John. Conversation was languid as the heat lessened. When it was cooler we changed into tennis clothes and drove to the Tanjong Malim Club.

The road through the rubber trees came out to the village, past the little hospital and over the bridge where brown-skinned women were washing clothes at the river bank. The village was crowded at this hour. Chinese, Indians and Malays sauntered along the street and in and out of the shops which were colourful, advertising their wares in English, Chinese and Arabic. The coffee houses were full. In the warmth of the late afternoon the aroma of Turkish coffee blended with the smell of ripe fruits and curry spices on the street stalls.

Over the level crossing was Tanjong Malim Station where cannas were planted in tidy flower beds by the platform, like any village station in England. Many of the waiting travellers were squatting on their haunches with oriental patience for a train that might not arrive till the following day. Beyond the railway were the grounds of the Sultan Idris College with extensive playing fields. It was a University for the sons of wealthy Malays, run on English lines, and the only one in Malaya.

From the other side of the bamboo hedge surrounding the Club was the noise of racquets hitting balls and the voices of the tennis players. Spectators sat round in rattan chairs sipping drinks. In the club house was one large room downstairs containing a billiard table, a well-thumbed piano and the bar. Upstairs was the lounge, bridge tables stacked in one corner and more rattan chairs whose cushions were covered in faded chintz. A table was set out with month-old copies of the *Tatler*, *Illustrated London News* and other English periodicals.

We stayed at the club till daylight had gone. Returning through the darkness it was reassuring to see the bungalow, lights streaming across the lawn, and Hi Ho in a fresh white coat waiting to serve dinner. Afterwards, on the verandah, a multitude of insects from the garden fluttering round the lamps, the day ended. Sometimes the cry of a wild animal wandering in the not-so-distant jungle sounded in the night. I only heard the less fearful sounds – the hum of the generator, the whine of mosquitoes, or the raucous croak of a bullfrog that went on till morning.

Everyone in the district was hospitable and mixed regardless of age. At this time the younger planters had not been allowed to go back to Britain and join the armed forces as some had wanted to do. After September 1939 the production of rubber and tin had been ruled as essential war work. Most young men were in the local volunteers. Having been brought up in an all female household, I had not met many young men before. Now there was an abundance of them. For the few girls there was no shortage of tennis partners for the mixed doubles, or escorts for the weekly dances in Kuala Lumpur.

I remember occasions, rare and formal, when Asians and Europeans met socially. There was Sports Day at the Sultan Idris College where mostly I met Malays. A yearly dinner party was given by Mr Song Mo Hin, the Chinese storekeeper, for his European customers, when he provided a special Chinese menu with sharks' fins, birds nest soup, and little ducklings roasted in a delicious way.

Mark John's clerk was Indian, a Brahmin, who sometimes entertained us for tea in his small bungalow in Tanjong Malim. Bespectacled and erudite, he received us with extreme courtesy while his wife served little cakes covered in bright pink sugar.

On special feast days the Tamil labourers all came to Escot bungalow and gave an entertainment on the lawn. We sat regally on a row of chairs and applauded while they performed strange dances, wearing fantastic costumes and weird masks.

I enjoyed meeting so many people. Sometimes I was shy and

tongue-tied, at other times over-exuberant. The humid heat affected neither my energy nor my appetite.

Buttons was more of a social success than I was. Only sixteen, very beautiful, she caused much amusement with her youthful high spirits. Though painfully aware of my puppy fat, more than anything I enjoyed the dances. Old or young, however unattractive, any man who asked me to be his partner was gladly accepted so that I could trip round the floor to the sound of a foxtrot or a waltz, whether it came from the dance band at the Selangor Club, the radiogram or a wind-up gramophone.

I loved the extravagant Malayan countryside with its fervent growth, the exotic flowers and fruits, the many birds and insects, and the vast areas of jungle hardly penetrated by man. I loved the rain too with the drama of heavy storms that came from Sumatra with a sudden rush of hot wind followed by seconds of utter calm. Then came the deluge which thundered down on the roofs of the bungalow and transformed the earth into myriads of little lakes and rivers. So soon afterwards the sun came out leaving the land cleansed and steaming.

With the agreement of the Malays for British advice and protection, the inhabitants – white-skinned, yellow and varying shades of brown – lived in comparative harmony, still keeping the language, dress and customs of the countries from which they had come. I saw nothing unacceptable in the colour barriers. The British had built roads, railways, bridges and schools in Malaya. They had set up a medical service and there was a fair operation of law and order.

The Empire seemed indestructible.

As the weeks went by the news from Europe got worse and worse. The Germans occupied the countries of Europe, then came the British evacuation of Dunkirk and the fall of France. Arrangements were made for Pippa and Susan to come out to Malaya. By the end of July they had sailed, their ship taking the long route round South Africa as the Suez Canal was closed.

Anne in the Cameron Highlands.

By now I had got restless living on the estate and I wanted to get a job. Of course I had no training of any sort but I answered an advertisement for a temporary receptionist at the Smoke House Inn in the Cameron Highlands – and to everyone's surprise I got the job. Several people had applied and it was assumed that a more mature person would get it.

The Cameron Highlands had only been opened up in the last few years as a hill station, and the approach was a road cut through jungle which began winding uphill near Ipoh and continued tortuously for forty miles with hairpin bends at every hundred yards. As it went higher the air became cooler and views of steep hillsides, flame of the forest trees scarlet among the dense foliage, appeared through gaps by the way.

At the top the jungle was being cleared and the hill station was developing. There were two hotels, the Smoke House Inn, a golf course, two schools for European children and a number of houses that could be rented for a holiday period. A few permanent residents were making a home there, preferring to retire in Malaya where they had lived for most of their lives rather than return to a Britain which they hardly knew.

It was nice to see English flowers. Roses, dahlias, asters and other summer varieties were growing in the gardens as well as Australian ones. It was good too, to feel the need for tweed skirts and sweaters again.

Many of the houses were built round the golf course and the Smoke House Inn was one of them. It aimed to create the atmosphere of an English country pub, built with mock oak beams and lattice windows. The bar was decorated with horse brasses and poker work and other reminders of English rural life. In spite of these attempts it did not succeed. Somehow the effect was too contrived. It was expensive to stay in one of the four bedrooms but the bar was open to all and everybody staying in the Highlands came in there.

Mrs Warin was a tiny woman who ran the place most efficiently. She needed someone to help her while her husband was away for a couple of months and I suspect she chose me as the most malleable of the applicants for the job. I took the bookings, made up the bills and generally looked after the guests. There was no domestic work except to arrange flowers. It was very easy. Though I muddled the bookings, added the bills incorrectly and made many other errors, Mrs Warin and I stayed on friendly terms. She was patient and I was eager to

Mrs Warin, Anne and Tony Warin.

please, and the fact that I was the only person who could control her lively five-year-old son probably contributed as much as anything to the guests' well-being. The people who stayed, mostly middle-aged couples, were always kind and tolerant about my mistakes. I enjoyed their comings and goings and the flow of people in the bar.

My afternoons were free. There was little I could do with them. The main recreation in the Highlands was golf and I borrowed three clubs and tried to learn the game. There were few players who wanted to go round the course with me so I had little chance to practise.

Mostly I went for walks, with the spaniel Smokey, through forest paths with ferns and mosses growing thickly on either side and sometimes crossing fast flowing streams. I discovered interesting plants like the Venus fly trap and I picked wild flowers that did not grow on the plains. At the highest point on the Highlands, reached by a long walk up a steep path, the trees were cleared at a panoramic viewpoint. All round were jungle-covered peaks except where a long valley of cone-shaped hills stretched westwards to the plains. Beyond was the sea. The light was ever-changing, colouring the clouds and forests with shades of blue and violet. It was breathtaking. I could have come to Shangri-la.

It was at the Cameron Highlands that I first met Gerry whom I married six years later.

He came into the Smoke House late one evening with another engineer from the Shell Company. Though I should have been on duty for another quarter of an hour I had already gone upstairs to bed as the bar was empty and I did not think anyone else would come in that day. It was annoying to hear voices below, and I threw on a dress and came downstairs, hoping to make a token appearance with no social pressure made on me.

Gerry and Bob had just arrived in the Highlands for their local leave and were in a party mood, insisting that I have a drink with them. I was only conscious of my half-buttoned dress and nothing else on underneath it, and I sat awkwardly with my drink until I could say goodnight.

It was not an auspicious beginning to a life-long association but during the rest of their leave they often came to the Smoke House and I spent some happy evenings with them. Bob was the quieter one, Scottish and serious. Gerry had a more dominant personality. He also had great charm and could talk easily to anyone he met. I was attracted to him although his self-confidence awed me. On leaving the Highlands he suggested we meet if ever I came to Singapore. But I did not think I would see him again.

September had ended when I left the Cameron Highlands and went back to Tanjong Malim. By then the Battle of Britain had been fought and won and the London blitz was beginning. In Kuala Lumpur there were more British servicemen about and the Selangor Club was full of army officers. I heard little concern about war in Malaya and felt very confident that the country was well-prepared for any Japanese attack – if it came at all.

Pippa and Susan had arrived at Escot after their long sea voyage. Books, tennis racquets and gramophone records were strewn about the verandah. In the bedrooms clothes lay in and out of trunks. A black puppy named Hamish was running around with a lot of affection lavished on him. The tennis court had been newly marked out and on another part of the lawn a badminton court had been set up. Other children from England had also come out to the district and there was a spate of picnics and parties for them all.

I remember there was great happiness at Escot then. After the separations of the last ten years Mark John and Dorothy were together again with all their family around them. The war news from Britain reported air raids on London, reducing houses to rubble in streets so familiar to us, and our anxieties were for the people there. But at Escot my parents felt secure, thankful that they and their children were in this peaceful place in the heart of Malaya, with no further separations foreseen.

In the garden the bulbul sang, his song like water cascading over stones, the temple tree shed its white blossoms on the grass, and the morning dew left glistening tear drops among the petals of the canna flowers.

Before long I had become restless again and kept asking my parents to let me take a secretarial course so that I could get a war job. Pitman's College in Singapore was about the only place where I could go, and my father agreed to let me start in the New Year.

After that I could talk of nothing else. I would certainly be able to do war work there. The colony of Singapore was considered the most

A water colour painting of Escot.

important British possession in the Far East. Known as the 'Impregnable Fortress', the heavy traffic of arms and men arriving on the island was continually in the news. Singapore was the capital of the Straits Settlements and the seat of government for the administration of Malaya.

In this city where so much was happening I felt I was sure to enjoy myself. It was reputedly a place to have a good time – especially if one was young, female and unattached. I was now old enough to live on my own, I insisted – although Ma had doubts about this. A boarding house within walking distance of Pitman's College was found for me and I waited impatiently for the days to pass.

Christmas 1940 was a good one and the last our family were to spend together for many years.

The bungalow was full with every spare bed and divan occupied for several young army officers were spending their leave at Escot. There was little elbow room at the long dining table to eat traditional turkey and Christmas pudding. Afterwards the verandah was cleared for party games and dancing to music from the radiogram.

On Boxing Day a rafting party had been organised. This special Escot entertainment was a merry occasion – as it always had been over the years – and ended the festivities.

The year ended – and with it my time in Malaya. So much had been new and yet so little had changed since I had been a child. So much had I enjoyed in this country I found very beautiful.

On the 1st January 1941, I took the night train to Singapore.

Chapter Five

As the carriages rolled slowly over the bridge across the Johore Causeway, the sea was shimmering in the early morning sunshine. Through the window of my sleeper I could see the marshy ground of Singapore's northern shore approaching. I was sure a wonderful future was beginning.

My new address was in Oxley Rise, a road on high ground near the centre of the town. It was a quiet road which ran from Orchard Road to Clemenceau Avenue, curving gently round the hill. All the houses in the road were boarding houses; they were too large to be used for anything else. Each one was surrounded by a large garden. They had been built in the early days of Singapore's development and now their huge rooms had made them unsuitable for private homes. The Mansion – a most appropriate name – was at one end standing on a mound by itself. It was a square house, two storeyed with a magnificent portico and wide shuttered windows. As the taxi drove up the gravel drive I wondered if it had originally been built for some rich merchant prospering in the days of Stamford Raffles.

In spite of the grandiose architecture, inside the atmosphere was no different from any English boarding house. The cavernous interior leading from the entrance hall revealed guests eating breakfast at separate tables. The smell of bacon made me hungry.

Upstairs, around the dining room, was a gallery and most of the bedrooms opened on to it. The landlady, Mrs Matthews, showed me to mine. Her flat pale face was unsmiling and her Mancunian accents did not respond to my gush of appreciation but I hardly noticed her as I viewed the room.

It was one of the cheaper ones, narrow and rectangular – almost a passage – but with a very high ceiling. It was part of an exceptionally large room partitioned several times. The minimum necessities were provided: a cheap wooden dressing table, a too-small wardrobe, one chair and a bed with a sparse canopy of mosquito netting. There was a little square of coconut matting on the floor. The window looked out on to a thick bamboo hedge behind which the servants' quarters were not quite obscured.

I could see no imperfections. It was a room of my own, not shared with a sister, and it was all I wanted.

At the table allotted to me another girl was eating breakfast.

Her name was Ricky, she told me, and she had come out from England on her own. She was working at Fort Canning, the Army HQ, which was nearby.

'The Mansion's not such a bad place,' she laughed. 'A bit crazy sometimes. My room's taller than it's wide. The house has been divided to make as many bedrooms as possible. But it's cheaper than the other boarding houses and the food's quite good.'

I told her about my family and Escot Estate and how I wanted to get a war job. 'I'm so excited at being here,' I told her. 'I've been longing to come to Singapore.'

'You'll have a marvellous time. There are always masses of parties and never enough girls to go round. You can go dancing every night of the week.'

She was vivacious and friendly and it was great fun to be with her. We shared our meals at The Mansion for the next ten months. I was lucky that I met her then for, in spite of my emphatic wish to be independent, it would have been lonely at The Mansion in those first weeks. Instead, I had someone a little older than myself with whom to share experiences and ask advice.

Pitman's College was only a short distance away in River Valley Road, and after breakfast I walked down the hill to start my secretarial course. I did not see it in the same rosy light that I had seen everything else that morning. It was a drab place with stuffy classrooms packed with old typewriters but I was glad to have the chance to work at something after a year's break from school. The Principal was a dour Scot; the rest of the staff were Asian. I was the only European student. My classes were held in the morning, my afternoons were free.

Too excited that day to stay still and regardless of the hot sun beating down, I went out after lunch to see what I could of the town. I walked down the slope of Oxley Rise and crossed a main road where trams rattled past and looked up at the hill where Fort Canning stood. Figures in khaki were walking in and out of the building over which flew the Union Jack. I walked along wide roads lined with grass verges and palm trees, past the Raffles Institute and other large white Government buildings – reminders of British officialdom – and continued till I crossed the iron bridge over the Singapore River. On the foetid water thousands of sampans were moored, tightly packed together, and the occupants – fishermen and their families – lived on these small boats with the ever present sour smell of human excreta and rotting fish.

I was suddenly in Chinatown. The North Bridge Road was a street of shops. Garish signboards advertised their wares and poles hung with washing extended from the upper windows of narrow frail houses. The acrid smell from the deep, wide gutters was strong. In the dark interiors, customers fingered jade and ivory pieces, delicate porcelain and bales of Shantung silk, and inspected camphor wood chests or tried on finely embroidered slippers.

Nearby the streets were Indian. There the shops sold exotic material for saris, trays of Benares brass and small tables of intricately carved teak.

I was ready to be enchanted with everything I saw. Returning across the bridge, exhilarated with wandering the streets and rubbing shoulders with the passers-by, Singapore seemed a romantic place, a city of East and West where people of all races lived and worked together.

It was a city greatly concerned with commerce. War had not troubled it for over a hundred years and during that time trade from the rich resources of Malaya had flourished. The sale of copra, spices, tapioca, sage and tinned pineapples had increased and the war in Europe had now accelerated the exports of tin, rubber and coconut oil to a more frantic rate than ever before.

Although peopled by many races Singapore could not be called cosmopolitan The communities did not mix nor did they all feel a special allegiance to the British Crown. The threat of attack did not unite this population – racial attitudes and differing loyalties insulated these communities from each other.

Eurasians held white collar jobs, superior to labourers but without the same status as Europeans. There were some wealthy families with Portuguese names that dated back to an earlier invasion of Malayan shores. The Chinese were the richest community, and the largest: successful businessmen who helped the growing numbers of refugees from the war in China. The Malays tended to live a rural life taking little interest in commerce. The majority of Indians were poor but able to make a better living than in India. A number of Japanese on the island were hard working and polite, many of them owners of small businesses such as photography or hairdressing. These occupations gave excellent scope for espionage, a fact ruefully remembered in later months.

The British were the administrators. There were civilians, government officials and businessmen, who had run Singapore before the outbreak of war, and now there were the increasing numbers of Army, Navy and Air Force personnel rapidly transforming the island into a garrison.

Over the years of increasing prosperity in the Colony a very high standard of living had developed for the European community. The enervating climate encouraged an easy life, and the women, particularly, had a great deal of leisure.

Hospitality was lavish and most of it was purely social. There was little cultural entertainment. Concerts were few and the only English theatre was the occasion when the Amateur Dramatic Society performed at the Municipal Hall. The Malayan Broadcasting Corporation was a small unit which had to cater for different tastes. Listening to the radio, except for news broadcasts, was not a normal way of spending an evening. The colour bar was rigid and few Europeans took an interest in the cultures of Asia.

Outdoor recreations were popular. The Cricket Club, the Yacht Club and the Golf Club were well-subscribed. So was the Swimming Club with its magnificent pool near the seashore where there was always a cooling breeze. In the green suburb of Tanglin where European homes in large well-tended gardens were hidden behind high hedges, was Tanglin Club. A pleasant place surrounded by trees, it was small but exclusive for it was expensive and old Singapore residents made admission difficult.

I was eager to join the social whirl. It was easy for a young English girl – a few introductions led to many invitations.

As Ricky had told me, there were lots of parties. Tennis parties, dinner parties, moonlight parties by the seashore, more formal parties at Government House – I accepted every invitation. I went to parties in the Officers' Mess at Changi, at Nee Soon, at the Air Force Bases and to dances at Singapore's Naval Base.

I enjoyed sailing, exploring little islands round Singapore which were no more than mangrove swamps. Some Sundays a party of us would drive to the east coast of Malaya and picnic on beaches of pure white sand stretching for miles, and where the thick vegetation grew down to the shore.

A single girl was welcomed as a member of Tanglin Club, paying only a nominal subscription, and I spent many afternoons there by the pool.

I met a great many people, though only in a superficial way. My immaturity and the circumstances of living on my own did not make closer friendships.

The married women were to be envied, I thought, secure with husbands and children. I watched them as they played their games of bridge and mahjong in the clubs or sat round the swimming pool, and I admired their self-confidence. Some always had young men around them ready to dance attendance and take them out in the evening.

There were not a large number of places for Singapore socialites to go but they were well-patronised and I had soon been to them all. Raffles Hotel which was often nearly empty in the daytime came to life in the evening when the dining tables, thick among the potted palms, were lit with individual lamps and the dance floor was full of evening dresses and colourful Mess uniforms. The orchestra played the hit tunes that London had heard in earlier months – we jogged up and down to the beat of 'In the Mood' or swayed to the lilt of 'Begin the Beguine'.

Most restaurants were expensive and some made the most of a romantic setting. Up at the Gap, a stony hillside outside the town, was a solitary café, no more than a hut, that overlooked the sea. Even if the food was not very good the tables set out in the open commanded a view of the coastline lit by moonlight, and the music of a Hawaiian band enhanced the illusion of a tropical paradise.

The cinemas which showed films in English – there were only three of them – were the only places to be air-conditioned. The largest one was in the Cathay Building, the one 'skyscraper' at that time in Singapore. Eight stories high, there were offices and flats and a restaurant above the cinema. Special performances of the latest film release were shown here in aid of the war effort. It was a social occasion when 'Buy a Bomber' girls – Singapore socialites – sold programmes. Everyone wore evening dress and the event was fully reported next day in the gossip column of the *Malay Tribune*.

Among the junior officers who took me out, many could not easily afford the high prices. Some, who had come from the fighting in North Africa or from the austerity of Britain, were glad to have been posted to Singapore. Others were scathing of this society and the continual round of pleasure at a time when Britain was at war.

Other Ranks were seldom invited to the houses of European civilians and many of them, living in barracks and far away from their homes, had little opportunity to talk to English girls. Dances for them were sometimes organised. These were lively evenings when as many girls as possible were mustered and we gathered in a big hall hired for the occasion. While the band played throughout the evening with a loud thumping beat, every girl had partners. No sooner did a waltz finish than, gasping for breath and giddy from being spun round and round, she would be grabbed by another soldier, sailor or airman to dance an energetic foxtrot. The evening came to an end and we all stood on our bruised and aching feet to sing 'God Save the King', our dresses wringing wet with perspiration. There was little time for conversation, no chance of hearing anything above the noise and little chance of getting to know anyone.

Later on during my stay in Singapore I used to go to an Other Ranks' club and I realised what a poor time most of these men had when off duty. There were clubs for them and efforts made for their welfare but compared to their officers they had a second-rate existence. Dancing for them usually meant a visit to the Happy World and money spent on 'taxi girls'.

To do something for the war effort I joined the Blood Group Unit. They were a small number of volunteers, all women, who were responsible for stamping the correct blood group of each serviceman on his identity disc. One afternoon a week we were collected in an army bus and driven to one of the Service establishments on the island. There we set up testing facilities on a long trestle table while the men were lined up to have a finger pricked for a blood sample. There were always a great many to do in the time and we prided ourselves on our speed and efficiency. Each of us had her allotted jobs. As I was the youngest, mine was the most energetic and the least responsible. I rushed up and down from one end of the long table to the other, taking drops of blood on slides for testing and then bringing back the result for stamping on the serviceman's disc. The heat and my enthusiasm usually left me exhausted by the end of the afternoon.

There were few evenings when I did not go out. There was little to do in The Mansion if I stayed in for there was no lounge in which to sit. Unless Ricky was in too I stayed in my bedroom and read a book.

At the end of March my parents wrote to say they were sending Buttons to join me. Ma sent detailed instructions to look after my younger sister, and at first I grumbled at the responsibility. But when she arrived, as excited as I had been, I was glad that she had come. Our meal times with Ricky became hilarious affairs, provoking even a faint smile from Mrs M. as she passed our table.

It was about this time, too, that I left Pitman's College, my course unfinished. I had mastered the theory of shorthand and had become bored with practising speeds every day. The Principal remonstrated with me but I was impatient to leave the dusty classrooms and was quite confident I could cope with a job. I had already been offered one.

War correspondents were beginning to come to Singapore and a Combined Services department working closely with the Ministry of Information had recently been formed to assist these correspondents, mostly from the British, Australian and American press. 'Services Public Relations Office' was to be their official link with the Services, helping them with information on Service matters, organising visits to guarded areas and, in the event of war, conducting them to the front line.

The establishment needed a secretary. For security reasons only European girls were considered suitable for work connected with the Services and, as there were so few of us, it was not difficult for me – even so inadequately trained – to get the job. Nobody else was available for it.

The elderly Commander RN who was to be the head of SPRO interviewed me. He smiled benignly when I told him I had no previous experience – which must had been obvious – and said that neither had he.

The staff included, besides the Commander and myself, a Lieutenant RNVR, once a reporter on the *Daily Mirror*, and an army photographer. The office was on the top floor of Union Building on Collier Quay and I was allotted a small room which overlooked the sea.

The Commander was right when he said he had no experience of Public Relations. He had retired from the Navy many years before and since then had been living in Fiji. Burly and blue-eyed, he had spent much of his life at sea. It was easier to imagine him on the bridge of his ship than to see him at his desk. He was totally unsuited to the job, knowing little about the press world, and the correspondents were often indignant at his lack of understanding. They complained of severe censorship of their reports and of information withheld from them. They were also contemptuous of material issued from GHQ, dismissing it as propaganda. News released for them was always worded in the most optimistic way as it could be picked up by local newspapers, and the confidence of the other populations was considered very important. There was also a Japanese press in Singapore which created problems in releasing information.

The Commander was disciplined, rigidly adhering to his directive from the Service Chiefs. The correspondents were younger, active men. Though aware of the necessity for security, they were frustrated that, in this island so much an area of world interest, they were able to get little real news. The liaison was not an amicable one.

My work included the Commander's letters, typing official handouts, organising a filing system and generally making myself useful.

At first I was not aware that I was particularly inefficient. The

Commanders and the others treated me with kindly resignation; it was difficult to replace me. I had not worked in any other office before and there was no previous girl to show me the ropes. I seldom arrived on time, my filing system was haphazard and my poor shorthand led to letters constantly being retyped. I had little understanding of the secret documents which passed so carelessly through my hands. The ancient Gestetner machine for official handouts left my fingers stained with black ink and produced smudged and unreadable copies. Some of the correspondents received them politely, others at once tossed them in my waste paper basket. Often they had already acquired the information contained in them.

Perhaps I spent too much time gazing out of the window. Below was a wonderful view of the waterfront. There were always little crafts on the sea, motor boats, junks, sampans, the men in them busy with their various pursuits. And on the horizon bigger ships were passing on their way to ports all over the world.

The wide main road ran along the shoreline towards the Cathedral and the Cricket Club. Vehicles of all kinds sped past – old cars, modern cars, bicycles too. Yellow taxis were rushing to their destinations. There were large American limousines driven by Malay chauffeurs, small Austin Sevens packed beyond capacity with Asian families, army trucks, ancient lorries on their way to market loaded with pineapples, crates of fish and other Singapore produce. Rickshaw men pulled their passengers, legs with knotted muscles moving at a fast trot.

Some of the correspondents I remember more than others. Ian Morrison of the *The Times*, tragically killed a few years later in Korea, was a quiet young men with a dry sense of humour, O.D. Gallagher of the *Daily Express* was my conception of a wild Irishman. There was Laurence Impie of the *Daily Mail*, Kenneth Selby-Walker of Reuters, and Harold Guard of Associated Press who was much older than the others. Also memorable was Cecil Brown of Columbia Broadcasting whose broadcasts to the USA on the inadequacy of Singapore's defences and the complacent attitude of the British caused acrimony in SPRO. He was a bad-tempered man and many of the things he said were attributed to this – although subsequent events did prove he was right.

But all the correspondents were kind to me and I found them interesting and amusing people. They grumbled, teased, or took me out to lunch, and I enjoyed working among them.

There were no pressures. It was a totally carefree existence for an eighteen-year-old. I ran up as many bills as I dared from Chinese and Indian tailors who made full-skirted evening dresses that billowed on the dance floor. Usually I chose styles too old for me, tottering on high heels and affecting a long cigarette holder.

Life was fun – until I fell in love. Then Singapore really became the wonderful place I had imagined when I stepped so eagerly from the train at the beginning of the year.

Walking down Oxley Rise one afternoon I met Gerry again. He lived there too, at the other end of the road. We were surprised that we had not met before, especially as our offices too were side by side on Collier Quay. From then on his two-seater MG stopped at the end of The Mansion drive each morning and each evening he brought me back again.

I began going back to tea with him. His small flat was on the first floor of another large house. I liked its stark white walls, black wood furniture and the divan with the red linen cover. A radiogram was in one corner, records tidily stacked. Everything was uncluttered. Coming in to the flat from the harsh sunlight and abundance of colour outside, the austere effect was restful. We had tea on the verandah where, through a row of tall tamboosu trees, was a view of orange-tiled roofs.

Gradually we spent all our available time together. We walked after tea in the wooded area beyond the Reservoir or among the colours and scents of the Botanical Gardens. Sundays became lazy days beside Tanglin pool and, when we did not go out into the town's night life,

Gerry by the swimming pool.

we spent evenings in the flat listening to music. We drove late at night very fast around the island in the little sports car, my long hair streaming in the wind, up to the Gap or to the top of Bukit Timah to look down on the lights of the town.

Sometimes we went through the old part of Singapore where the streets were narrow and over-populated dwellings of wood and brick were flimsily built. It was the district of prostitution and opium dens and other vices of an eastern port. To my eyes the scene was picturesque but the smell of squalor was there and some of the inhabitants ugly with disease. Once I persuaded Gerry to stop for a short while at a hotel unpatronised by Europeans. I had been disappointed not to find a more cosmopolitan atmosphere in Singapore. In Tanjong Malim there had been at least some involvement in the lives of the Asians around me. Here I had no such contacts. There was nothing remarkable about the colourless hotel room, stuffy with the odour of burnt out joss sticks and furnished with little else but a spitoon and a bed with a hard bolster but, for me, it was another glimpse of this city whose polyglot peoples had lives so different from my own.

Gerry had hated Singapore when he first came out from England in 1939. He had never felt really well in the humid climate and, homesick, he had drunk too much in the first months. Though committed to stay till the end of the war, he did not intend to renew his contract again with Shell. Since his exemption from the Volunteers for Special Duties, he had started working as a relief announcer at the studios of the Malayan Broadcasting Corporation for some evenings of the week. This work was new to him, he enjoyed it, and life had become tolerable.

We talked about England, about places we knew, remembering nostalgically lights in Piccadilly, red London buses and foggy November evenings. He told me about his home in London and his days as an engineering student. I was fascinated by stories of life in a bed-sitter of a young man, well-educated and without money, living in the London of the thirties.

Attractive to other girls – and to older women too – he was different from other young men I knew. When he was enjoying himself he was twice as alive as anyone else, and I was enthralled with him.

My upbringing had not included much enlightenment on sex, religions other than Christianity nor on the social evils of the day. Politics in my family were traditionally conservative. My knowledge of the world was mostly gleaned from works of fiction – good and bad – which I read copiously.

So when he talked I listened. I wanted to learn all I could. Eight years older than me, he had vivid powers of description and a clear analytical brain which caused me to question much that I had accepted before. Sometimes I argued with him but I usually lost, for my views were unformed and my reasoning powers hardly used.

I began to see life around me with a new understanding which was more stimulating than anything I had yet experienced. Wholly romantic, it was an awakening of mind and body.

Of course Gerry found me naive. But as the weeks passed he began to feel a responsibility which he had not known with other girls.

The Japanese invaded Indo China that July and the threat of war increased. They now had airfields from which to bomb Singapore and a Naval Base only a few hundred miles away. But for most European civilians there was no feeling of imminent danger. The heavy flow of propaganda encouraged this confidence. In the newspapers there were always notices of army manoeuvres, naval exercises, reports of more troops arriving from Britain, from Australia, from India. Men in uniform were everywhere. Planes flew overhead all day and from the south shore the sound of the big guns at the Naval Base were often heard.

Another factor in the illusion of security was the jungle. Covering much of the Malayan Peninsula, it was considered impossible for an enemy to penetrate.

At night searchlights lit up the sky, the sirens were regularly tested and a 'brown-out' practice was enforced for a hour or so. No shelters had been built and there was little to remind anyone of the horrible realities of an air raid. Concern for the bombing of cities in Britain was more in our minds than fear of an attack on Singapore.

In September the British Government sent out Alfred Duff Cooper to report to Whitehall on the defence position. The number of war correspondents increased and more staff arrived for SPRO. One of these officers was Major Fisher who took over much of the Commander's work. He was a man in his late thirties who had seen service in the Abyssinian campaign and in the Middle East and, coming from Britain, which was now highly geared to an all-out war effort, he was very critical of the complacent attitudes he found in Singapore.

He was also critical of my poor efforts and I struggled to improve. I went back to Pitman's College for a weekly evening class but it made little difference to my ability to read back my shorthand or type without mistakes.

Buttons, whom I had completely neglected in these last months, had abandoned the Pitman's course after an even shorter time than I had done and, with Ricky's help, was working in Fort Canning in the filing room. As we had both got war jobs my father had not objected very much to the waste of the fees.

Ricky came with us when we went back to Escot for a long weekend. Once again we travelled on the night train. The estate seemed a sleepy place after Singapore. Pippa and Susan had gone away to school in the Cameron Highlands and only Hamish barking excitedly disturbed the quiet of the afternoon. My parents were delighted to have daughters in the bungalow again and welcomed Ricky.

She was getting married in the near future to Paddy, a man in the Malayan Police whom she had met only three months before. Her home would be in a district of Johore and as she had not seen much of Malaya, we wanted to show her all we could of Tanjong Malim.

In spite of the fun of homecoming, I was preoccupied with my Singapore life, counting each hour till I could go back. But as we drove away in the midday heat I looked back at the rambling old bungalow. The sun shone fiercely on its faded green roofs and the peeling paint on the downstairs windows. The lowered sunblinds along the verandah hid the familiar interior and gave the house a secretive look. The air was heavy. No leaves stirred in the enclosing rubber nor in the garden where the colours were as intense as ever. It seemed so still that for a moment I felt it was unreal. If I closed my

Buttons, Anne and Ricky.

eyes it would disappear like a castle in a fairy story leaving only trees in a dark wood.

The car gathered speed along the drive and the bungalow was out of sight. I had no presentiment then that I would not see Escot again.

Ricky and Paddy were married in October. The wedding was a small and riotously happy affair. Buttons and I missed her. The Mansion was never the same afterwards.

Captain Steel had joined the staff at SPRO. He was the field officer who would conduct correspondents to the battle areas in the

Anne, Bob and Buttons at Puh Bukum.

event of war. Young and energetic, he had worked in Fleet Street in peacetime. Perhaps this made him more sympathetic towards the correspondents, with whom he was very popular. Otherwise their dislike of the Commander was now acute and they had nicknamed the department 'Aspro for Headaches'.

Although troops and equipment continued to pour into Singapore and the defence build-up was stressed almost every day in the newspapers, an imminent invasion was not expected at this time. The north west monsoon was beginning and it was assumed that the Japanese would not attempt any landing in Malaya until it ended in March.

Only in SPRO did I hear less optimistic voices. Not everyone in the office shared a confidence in the defence preparations and some doubted more loudly than others. Cecil Brown's broadcasts to America were getting violent and his words of doom would be picked up on radios all over Malaya. As this could affect morale – particularly of the Asians – he was constantly being checked by censorship and his clashes with authority were becoming frequent.

Another well-known journalist from the USA, Martha Gellhorn, paid a fleeting visit to Singapore, was lavishly entertained, and returned to write an article on the luxurious living of the British in spite of looming war clouds – criticism which was felt by her hosts to be unfair comment.

However, even the most serious doubters were silenced when, on 2nd December, two of Britain's biggest naval ships were sent to Malayan waters. The *Prince of Wales* and the *Repulse* sailed into the Naval Base to the sound of wildly cheering crowds waiting to greet them.

It was the main topic of conversation that week. At the office, in the clubs, over drinks at the bar, by the swimming pool, people were rejoicing. With these ships to guard us, everyone agreed, it might well deter the Japs from coming into the war altogether... and if they did attempt an invasion, well, we were ready for them.

Probably I was even less afraid of a Japanese attack than anyone. At this time I was living from day to day, absorbed in my first love affair. That there could be any change in this sublime state was impossible to contemplate. I hardly thought about a war at all.

Yet, when it came a few days later, it surprised everybody.

Chapter Six

On that last peaceful Sunday morning I sat by the pool at Tanglin and waited for Gerry.

The day was hot and cloudless and the swimmers splashed in the sunshine. Sunbathers were stretched out on rattan chaise longues, others sat with long cool drinks in the shade of the surrounding trees. In the clubhouse tables were laid and white coated 'boys' were waiting to serve lunch.

Eventually Gerry arrived, rather late. He had been on duty at the Malaya Broadcasting studios and he apologised, saying that just as he was going off the air a 'flash' message had come in and he had stayed to read it. A Japanese fleet had been sighted off the coast of Cambodia and was sailing in a westerly direction.

Over our curry we discussed the implications of this news.

I asked Gerry what it meant. 'I think it means,' he said, 'that if the Japs attack Thailand, the Thais would ask Britain for help and before very long we really would be at war with Japan.'

There was a placard which had been hanging in the Hong Kong and Shanghai Bank for the last few weeks. It read, 'The defences of Malaya have been tested and not found wanting.'

'The Air Force can deal with any invaders,' I cheerfully remarked, 'and if the Japs did land in Malaya, they wouldn't be able to get through the jungle – only monkeys can do that.'

The events taking place in the South China Seas seemed a long way from Singapore.

At the end of the afternoon the club was unusually empty. All officers had disappeared. One by one they had been recalled to their units. It must be another 'alert', we decided; there had been one or two recently.

It was after midnight when we separated on The Mansion steps. A full moon was shining over the rooftops, various buildings easily distinguished. Flashing lights over the cinema advertised Bob Hope and Dorothy Lamour in *The Road to Rio*.

I was in a deep sleep when four hours later the sirens woke me – shrill and frightening in the stillness of the hot night. Overhead the noise of aeroplanes was coming nearer...a series of explosions followed...one in a nearby street sounded very loud. My heart pounded furiously and I jumped out of bed and ran to the window. The sky was alive with searchlights moving urgently round the sky and anti-aircraft guns were firing.

Outside my bedroom door I could hear excited voices. People were coming out of their rooms and talking in the gallery. One voice, louder than the others, was insisting that this was only an Air Raid Practice and nobody need worry.

Buttons burst into my room and switched on the light.

'Turn it off,' I hissed at her.

'Everybody's got their lights on,' she retorted, 'and the street lamps in Oxley Rise are on too.'

'Those were real bombs, I'm sure. The war's begun.' I said.

We waited for the planes to return but they did not come back. After what seemed like hours the all-clear sounded and we went back to bed, wondering what the morning would bring.

By breakfast time the night's event were known. The Japanese had attempted a landing at Khota Bahru on the east coast of Malaya; attacks had been made on Hong Kong and Singora in Siam. More astounding was the news of the raid on the US fleet in Pearl Harbour.

The war had indeed begun.

At the bottom of The Mansion's drive Gerry was waiting and we drove to Collier Quay. The streets were deserted, with little traffic on the roads and there was no sign of devastation. But in Raffles Place the front of Robinson's stores had been blown in and other shops demolished.

The bombs were small ones but the destruction shocked me. I had never before seen the results of an explosion. Yesterday this had been a shopping centre – now it was an ugly sight. Glass and debris were everywhere, a hole gaped in the building and floors hung in mid-air. Here a man had met sudden death.

Looking at the bomb damage I arrived even later than usual at the office and the Major was waiting for me. He was angry. 'It is abominable that you can't be on time on this of all mornings,' he raged. 'There is an emergency of the first magnitude – telegrams have been pouring in. Why aren't you at your desk?' At first I looked at him, astonished. His eyes were blazing, his face drawn and tired for he had been up since two o'clock that morning. I had never seen him like this before. On other days he had ignored my unpunctuality.

I apologised, and retreated to my office to control the tears that suddenly came.

The Major's outburst was well-deserved and salutary. Once recovered in the privacy of my room I realised how lax my attitude had become. My past zeal to contribute to the war effort had gradually been diminished by other distractions in Singapore, and by the grumbles of the correspondents and their contempt for the department. Now I was glad to feel I was needed – despite my inadequacies.

I worked hard after that. Telegrams and memos went to and fro all day long, and people came in and out of SPRO discussing the new turn of events. There was a feeling of optimistic excitement. America with all her resources was in the war; she would fight against Germany as well as Japan, and Britain – alone for many months – now had a powerful ally.

I typed three official communiqués issued during the morning. One spoke of confused fighting taking place at Khota Bahru, the second stated that there had been Japanese landings in Thailand and the third reported raids on aerodromes in north Malaya. They did not contradict the impression that everything was going well and that British troops were coping successfully with the situation.

The newspapers, reporting on the night's raid, described the damage as negligible. The bombs were 'anti-personnel', making craters only six foot deep. The Press also stressed the absence of panic among the inhabitants of Singapore. European and Asian alike were starting their allotted jobs.

On that first day there was a tremendous confidence everywhere. The uncertainty was over. War had come and everyone was ready to play their part in winning it.

The second day brought the disaster that was a cause of Britain's defeat only ten weeks later.

Early in the evening, when many of us were having a drink before dinner, the announcement came through on the radio – the *Prince of Wales* and the *Repulse* were reported sunk three hundred miles away off the east coast of Malaya. It was almost impossible to believe this news. Only a week ago they had sailed so gloriously into Singapore's Naval Base. It was a sober evening as the optimism of the day ebbed and the gravity of the situation was realised.

Arriving at the office the following morning I found O.D. Gallagher at my typewriter. His eyes were bloodshot, his hair was matted with oil and he looked exhausted. He had been the accredited war correspondent on the *Repulse* and had been in the sea for several hours the previous day. His own machine had gone down with the ship and he was urgently writing his story.

Later in the week he broadcast his eye-witness account from the MBC studios. The battleships had left Singapore at dawn to deal with the Japanese fleet which was reported to be in the Gulf of Thailand. A few hours later enemy planes appeared off Kuantan and attacked the battleships. With no air cover and their guns totally unable to protect them from wave after wave of deadly precision bombing, they sank. The *Repulse* had keeled slowly over, oil pouring out and spreading a thick carpet on the sea around. Gallagher and many others had slid into the water and had floated until destroyers had eventually picked them up.

That was the first story of Japanese success. By the end of the week Penang had been captured and the enemy occupied northern Malaya.

In Singapore not many people at this time understood the serious situation. We believed these to be temporary setbacks: before long British forces with their superior strength must surely rally. But the ensuing weeks brought nothing but defeat until the final débâcle.

It seems strange in retrospect that we had so little foresight of how quickly the end would come. Only six hundred miles away there was chaotic fighting with British soldiers retreating and where military equipment, so often boosted in past months, was proving inadequate against Japanese tanks and guerilla warfare. It was not, as once anticipated, to be a war where the opponents fought face to face on the plains of Malaya. Soldiers were up against little men on bicycles, who wore gymshoes and dressed like friendly Asians, but who appeared unexpectedly from the hitherto 'impenetrable jungle' carrying automatic weapons. Early raids on airfields had destroyed many fighter planes and this shortage of air cover was a disastrous factor in the whole war.

Yet in Singapore almost normal life had returned to the island. A broadcast by the Governor had encouraged us to carry on 'business as usual'. As much as possible it was hoped to present an unruffled attitude to the situation which must inspire confidence in the other populations. The extra news bulletins and special announcements which came hourly in the first days of the war decreased, and the MBC put on new plays, concerts and special features. The local press had heartening comments on stories of the retreating troops which lessened the impact of the daily bad news. Even the *Malaya Tribune* continued to publish its gossip column.

There was no shortage of food, drink or petrol – even with a rationing system. There were no more air raids. It was impossible to black-out houses with their open verandahs, so lights were dimmed ready to be turned out completely at the sound of an alert. Once the hotels and clubs had complied with regulations they were full again. In Raffles I danced to the music as before though some of the usual faces were missing now that regiments had been sent to join the fighting. Those people who felt alarmed at the war news did not express their fears except in the privacy of their homes. It would be unforgivable to be called a defeatist.

In SPRO it was less hectic than that first day for most of the correspondents were away at the battle areas together with Captain Steel whose efforts and efficiency they all praised. I read their reports with eager interest. The Malayan war was headline news all over the world and I was pleased to be in the centre of it all.

My first deprivation was the loss of Gerry's regular company. The Volunteers had been called up, and Gerry's reserved occupation kept him on oil installations on the island. He had moved his room to a house outside the town at Astrid Park and he did not come into Singapore except in the evenings. Sometimes he worked at the MBC and had even been given his own programme, 'Puzzle Corner', based on a weekly BBC series. We met at infrequent and uncertain intervals. I had to be content with the sound of his voice blaring out of houses in the town on my long walk home in the evening. The programmes were popular, judging from the number of people who rang the MBC if they thought he had made a mistake.

Buttons and I decided to leave The Mansion and move to the Tanglin area where it was easier to find lifts to the office. Most of the houses in Cairnhill Road were like others in the suburb, secluded in their large gardens, but No. 39 was one of a short row of terrace dwellings inhabited by Asians. Sharing with a young RAF wife, we rented it from its Chinese owner. After the lofty rooms of The Mansion it seemed absurdly small. Two bedrooms upstairs only just held our possessions; there was one living room below and an outside kitchen and bath house. A Chinese amah – probably younger than we were – came early in the morning to cook and clean and stayed till late at night. We did not speak each other's language but joint efforts to communicate caused us all much amusement.

By European standards the little house was primitive but it was fun to have a place of our own, and behave in noisy fashion without incurring the disapproval of anyone.

The day before Christmas the air raids began again. They were more frequent this time, the planes coming two or three times in the night. Flying in tightly packed formation they were clearly visible in the rays of the searchlights. There were no fighters to intercept them and although anti-aircraft guns fired all the time I never saw a plane brought down.

At first we sheltered in a slit trench in Cairnhill Road, newly dug that week by civil defence workers. We did not feel it gave much protection as we gazed up at the bomber force flying over us undisturbed by ack-ack fire. It seemed difficult to realise they were a cause of destruction, for their bombs fell outside the town and none fell in the Tanglin district. Crouching uncomfortably in our nightclothes in this muddy ditch, we giggled with nervous bravado and suffered numerous bites from mosquitoes: stagnant water collecting in the bottom of the trench made an excellent breeding ground. After that night we never sheltered there again but stayed in our beds.

General unease that the Japanese had not been halted was increasing. Voices criticised the authorities. Questions as to why the Army had not been more prepared – why had no proper shelters been built – were being asked. There was grumbling at red tape and actions by Whitehall and indignation at racial discrimination after the evacuation of Europeans from Penang. In spite of cheerful news bulletins, Europeans and Asians alike were bewildered. When so much had been said about the strength of Malaya's defences – what was happening?

Stories of heroism circulated: of tough little Gurkha troops who fought with so much tenacity – of the endurance of the Surrey and the Leicester regiments who had been in the north when the attack began – of the bravery and skill of the Argyll and Sutherland Highlanders.

Always the stories were of soldiers with the odds against them. Previous British intelligence had deemed that tank warfare would not be possible in jungle terrain, yet enemy tanks were successfully pushing southwards. British troops were fighting without tanks, little air cover (many machines had been lost in the first days of the war), and against Japanese intelligence unnervingly accurate.

But reinforcements were rumoured to be arriving soon. Then, surely, we would hear of British victories instead of stories of retreat.

My memories of Christmas Day are of Tanglin Club at lunchtime. Extra tables had been laid and every place occupied. Colour filled the clubroom – green tropical foliage merged with blue and khaki uniforms, the variegated dresses of the women and dazzling white of starched clothing and napery. The Duff Coopers were among a party of senior officials at one end of the room. Many eyes gazed with admiration at Lady Diana who wore a beautiful picture hat. Evacuees from North Malaya, now homeless, swelled the numbers of people eating and drinking. Everyone was determined to be merry whatever the days ahead might bring.

I returned to the office, sleepy after Christmas fare shared with Gerry and others, finding it difficult to work in the heat of the afternoon.

It was a different sort of Christmas at Escot.

Pippa and Susan were home from the Cameron Highlands for the school holidays when the family woke one morning to hear on the radio that Britain was at war with Japan. Convoys of troop lorries began passing along the main road northwards to the fighting area. In those first days of the war Pippa and Susan had walked down the long drive through the rubber and had stood by the side of the road

Pippa, Buttons and Susan with Mark John at Escot.

to wave at them. The soldiers responded with loud cheers and victory signs – two young English girls were not a common sight. Later in the week, when Pippa and Susan were by the roadside, they saw lorries returning full of exhausted and wounded men who hardly noticed them any more.

Suddenly Tanjong Malim was full of European women and children from the north who had been evacuated from their homes, and everyone was finding beds for them. In Escot bungalow every possible space was made for these shocked women and children so suddenly uprooted from their homes.

After Penang fell there were rumours that all was not going well. Apart from radio bulletins there was no way of knowing what was happening. News was confused. Sometimes it was reported that the Japanese were quite far south, other stories said they were only at Taiping. This uncertainty was due to bands of Japs infiltrating the jungle, sometimes by river, and appearing south of British troops, instituting a pincer movement.

At night bombers flew over the bungalow. There were no warning sirens. Only the the whirr of their machines and the swinging of the electric lights in the ceiling warned of their passing.

The day before Christmas the telephone rang in the afternoon. It was the Captain of the Local Defence asking for Mark John. Ma explained that he had gone to Slim River to pay the coolies and give out the rice ration. The Captain was surprised. Did she know that all British civilians had already left Perak and Tanjong Malim was only a mile away from the border? He urged her to leave immediately. The British were regrouping and it was likely there would be a battle soon at Slim River.

The following day Ma and the girls left Escot. My father had arranged for them to stay with some friends in Johore. 'Just for the time being,' he said, trying to be cheerful. 'I don't suppose it'll be long before we are all back again.'

Susan looked round the bungalow as they prepared to go. Would there be fighting at Escot? she wondered. Would soldiers be shooting on the lawn or killing each other on the verandah and bumping into the furniture? It was quite exciting really, she thought – in a sort of way – and at least she was not going to be sent back to school.

With Hamish on a lead they arrived at Kuala Lumpur station just after an air raid when they watched the planes machine-gunning the train. When they were able to get on it, they were refused permission to take Hamish. Peacetime regulations still prevailed and, without a permit, Hamish was not allowed in Johore. Sadly he was left behind on the platform. Two British soldiers, seeing Pippa and Susan's tears, promised to look after him but, of course, he was not heard of again.

By 6th January the battle for Slim River was lost with terrible casualties on both sides. A day later Kuala Lumpur fell. The next defence line was to be along the Muar River in Johore.

Before long my family were among the refugees in Singapore. Ma and the girls had come on New Year's Day and Mark John had appeared ten days later. He had little money for his income was entirely tied up with the estates. He had stayed as long as he could, destroying stocks of rubber and burning fields of young trees before they could be used by the enemy. Finally he was ordered to go by the evacuating British army. He had left behind Asian people who had served him for many years and whom he loved. Yet had he stayed he could have done little for them – if not interned, he would have died by Japanese hands.

The servants had all gone to new homes in the village. Before he left Hi Ho had collected the silver and hidden it at the bottom of a well in the garden. The bungalow was abandoned. There was no shooting on the lawns, no hand-to-hand fighting under its roof, as Susan had imagined. It was merely looted of all its contents and stayed empty for the next four and a half years.

In Singapore it was becoming difficult to find somewhere to stay. Hotels and boarding houses were full, everyone made room for evacuees, emergency accommodation was organised by the civil authorities. Pippa and Susan were housed with friends, and my parents put up in a small flat in River Valley Road. It had been commandeered by SPRO and only used in the daytime and the Major, who was now running the department (the Commander had gone), allowed them to stay there. It was small and dirty but it was somewhere to sleep and unpack their suitcases. Ma was horrified to find bedbugs and collected one in a match box to show us.

When talking about the situation it was difficult to predict what would happen in the following months – or weeks perhaps. My parents decided that Pippa and Susan should be sent away, and accepted the suggestion of Ma's sister, our Aunt Moll, in Southern Rhodesia that they should stay with her until peace came. They must now get on the first available ship for South Africa.

Trying to get passages in the crowded shipping offices was a nightmare. It was impossible to say when the next boat for Africa would leave, my mother was told by an official, nor could he give her sailing dates for any ship at all. He advised her to keep applying every day until an Africa-bound ship came in.

My father, offering his services for civil defence, found he was useful to the Army in a special capacity. Many of the Tamil labourers at the docks, frightened by the air raids, had run away, and urgent cargo was lying on the quayside. The hurried building of shelters was also being delayed. Understanding this labour force and their language, he could speed this vital work. Younger planters who might have been employed were in the Volunteers, fighting in Malaya.

He was immediately commissioned with the rank of Captain in the RASC Pioneer Corps. At the age of sixty-one Mark John joined the Army for the first time.

He returned to River Valley Road wearing uniform and we all laughed at his appearance. It was apparent that stocks at the QM stores were running low. Nothing fitted him. His khaki shirt hung off his small frame and his shorts came lower than ever below his knees. He had not been issued with any weapon although he wore a holster.

His decision to sign on in the Army meant that he would receive pay and allowances and that his wife and children would have the advantages of an Army family. It meant, too, that, as an Army officer, he could not leave Singapore unless under military command.

The Muar Line had not held. 'After fierce fighting,' I typed out the communiqué, 'British troops were falling back to previously prepared positions.' Now the belief was that the great turning point of the campaign would take place in South Johore.

Cecil Brown's prophetic broadcasts had been banned. They were considered too dangerous for the morale of the Asian population. His accreditation papers had been withdrawn and he had gone back to America.

But opinion among European civilians was that, whatever else,

Singapore would hold. It must. Was it not one of the most fortified strongholds of the British Empire?

As the Japanese continued to advance through Johore we were – at first – insulated from some of the hideous results of the war.

There was enough to eat although there was not the luxury food obtainable a few weeks earlier. Servants continued to wait on us. There was no shortage of alcohol and we could still go out to dine and dance. Raffles Hotel and other places were usually crowded.

Air raids were now daily as well as nightly occurrences. But they were short and sharp and the planes, seldom checked by fighters, unleashed their bombs and soon went away. Moments of fear were shortlived; the all-clear sounded soon after the alert. The damage from the small bombs was accurately inflicted on military objectives on the island and sometimes on the Asian parts of the town. We knew there were too few fighters and we believed that the men who flew these out-of-date machines had their encounters away from the town to avoid aircraft falling in flames over the populated areas. Rumours of a consignment of Spitfires arriving any day were prevalent. The misery was at its worst when flimsy houses, over-crowded with Chinese and Indian families, collapsed into rubble, the number of deaths uncounted.

Stories from tired soldiers back from the fighting in Johore gave the truest indication of the strength of the Japanese. In Singapore we had not met the enemy face to face.

I heard of people I had known reported dead – killed in the jungle fighting during the past few weeks. Young men with whom I had played tennis or waltzed so light-heartedly around the dance floor were suddenly gone for ever. It was difficult to realise I should not see them again. Planters who had not left their estates in time were reported missing. My father's old friend, George Callard, had not been seen since the battle at Slim River. It was believed he was ambushed by Jap soldiers while walking along a path on his estate.

As I did not often go outside the city I saw little of the devastation.

My activities were concentrated between Cairnhill Road and SPRO, which had now moved the office to a flat in the Cathay Building. I knew little of what was really happening except from hearsay and official comment.

Sometimes I went to see my family at River Valley Road. I usually found Ma chatting to the odd member of SPRO staff who used the flat during the day. The air raids were a great ordeal for she reacted with the same uncontrollable terror she experienced during thunderstorms owing to a traumatic incident in childhood. Much to our embarrassment – especially in public places – at the sound of a siren she would dive under a table regardless of where she was. Being a large woman she was always very conspicuous when the British were trying to appear calm and indifferent to the explosions. Once the all-clear sounded she was immediately as composed as before.

There was still no ship for Africa and there were scores of people every day trying to get passages. A young woman ahead of Ma in the queue who was also trying to go to South Africa suddenly decided that as there was a ship leaving for Australia that day, she would go there with her baby. She offered to take Pippa and Susan with her. From there, she said, they could all go to South Africa and she would see that they arrived in Salisbury where Aunt Moll would look after them. Ma had to make an instant decision as there were others in the queue behind her – and she agreed to the suggestion. She felt that she should stay with her husband and Buttons and me, but to get her younger children away from the hazards of war she must let them them go with a comparative stranger to an unknown country and trust that they would eventually reach her sister. It was a difficult decision.

On 20th January Pippa and Susan left with Mrs Payne and her baby. Ma sent a cable to the Evacuation Reception at Sydney to receive them, saying that she would follow if the situation worsened.

It was just as well they went. The Japanese were nearly at the back door of Singapore.

Suddenly the bombing was much heavier. The raiders came more often and attacked the centre of the town and the residential areas, killing more civilians. From the upper floor of the Cricket Club I saw a bomb fall in the street outside. An old Chinese had just stopped his rickshaw, looking bewildered as the noise came nearer. A second later he was dead. The blast threw him across the road where he lay spreadeagled in the dust, blood trickling from his body. I had not witnessed death before.

Life became an attempt to carry on as usual regardless of new disasters occurring every day. We made plans for next week or the week after that but it was a waste of time to speculate if they would materialise. I saw Gerry at irregular intervals. He was working all day bringing stocks of gasoline and oil from the outlying islands to sumps in Singapore. Thousands of gallons of fuel were being brought in and stacked in unlikely places. Some nights he was firewatching at these dumps, and on many other evenings he was on duty at MBC studios at Thomson Road.

We did not have much time together. When we did it was difficult to be alone. We could only drive away and sit somewhere, often watching the night raiders in the light of the searchlights and listening to the sound of the ack-ack guns and exploding bombs.

No fear of defeat entered my head. I did not doubt that a siege of Singapore would end in a glorious victory. The island would defend itself heroically, enduring hardship until the enemy retreated – as the British had done in the blitz, the people of Malta, the Russians at Stalingrad or the Chinese in the cities of Chungking and Shanghai.

Nor was I afraid that I should not survive this experience. The heightened sense of being alive, the sharing of danger with others, living each hour without a thought for the next, excluded everything but a delirious happiness never to happen in my life again. I was on the crest of a high wave – sometime ahead the wave would break but that I could not imagine.

In the last days of January the mood of confidence that had

73

prevailed throughout the Malayan war changed overnight. Wednesday the 29th was a day like previous ones. Bombs fell, we went to our jobs as usual, morale was high and we felt sure that Singapore would hold out. By Thursday morning Churchill had made a speech in the House of Commons making it clear that no more reinforcements were to go to Singapore. Suddenly there was talk of evacuating all women not essential to the defence of the city. Major Fisher and the other staff left to set up SPRO in Colombo. Most of the correspondents left too and Captain Steel remained in charge.

In the evening my parents came to the house in Cairnhill Road. It was probable, my father told us, that two ships would be leaving the next day for the UK and the Government were giving free passages to women and children. He wanted Buttons and me to go on one of them. My mother would be leaving also but she was going to try and get to Sydney.

The thought of leaving Singapore was terrible to me. How could I leave at this time? I argued desperately. My job was important – it would be wrong to go and I wanted to stay. I swore nothing would induce me to leave. Though Ma made efforts to make me understand, I refused to listen and shut myself in my bedroom.

Later Gerry came to say goodbye. We drove to the end of Cairnhill Road and parked the car under a tree. The scent of frangipani was sickly sweet.

'You must go on that ship tomorrow,' he told me. 'There may not be another chance. The position is grim.'

The reality of the situation was dawning on me. I feared that I might never see him again.

'I want to stay with you,' I said frantically.

'You will only be a liability to your father and me. I shall try to escape. As a civilian I shan't have the protection of being a Prisoner of War and the Japs will probably shoot oil company engineers. If there is a surrender I shall get into anything that floats and make a dash for it. Then I'll find you again.'

We exchanged addresses in England and said goodbye.

The following morning I went early to the office, half hoping that I could evade my situation. But by lunchtime as I came down the steps of the Cathay building I saw my father coming towards me. He said that he was taking me back to the house where Ma and Buttons were already waiting. I was to pack a suitcase that I could carry myself and make a bedding roll. Then he would drive us to the docks. I opened my mouth to argue again but I saw the look in his eyes – gentle but firm – and I knew it was the end of Singapore for me.

Up in the bedroom I tried to pack. What should I take and what should I leave? I couldn't bear to leave the oyster satin dress behind. In the end I took the things I liked most with the result that my only suitcase was stuffed with evening dresses: satin, chiffon, taffeta was crushed in and more practical clothes were left behind in the wardrobe. My collection of Fats Waller records remained in the corner of the bedroom – even I realised that I could not carry them with me.

The road to the docks was a slow procession of cars taking families with their luggage and bedding rolls. We passed lorries going in the opposite direction carrying soldiers. They were reinforcements who had just arrived that morning in the ships which were to take us away.

The air raid siren went as we got out of the car. Planes appeared quickly and we all dived into a shelter – a long concrete trench with a roof recently built. We had just got in when a stick of bombs fell over the docks, one of them hitting the other end of the shelter. Fortunately that particular bomb killed nobody but all over the docks fires were starting.

It was here Buttons and I said goodbye to Ma who went off to the little office on the quay where an official was issuing passes. She said she would see us in England eventually when she had collected Pippa and Susan from Sydney.

As we approached our allotted ship, the *Duchess of Bedford*, dust was still settling round her stern. A bomb had just made a gash in her side. Already repairs were starting. The quayside was crowded with women and children embarking, and their men who were staying behind. Sweat poured off us as we struggled with our suitcases and bedding up the gangway. Around us were tense faces.

After my father had seen us on board he did not stay. My mother would be waiting for him. He gave us some travellers cheques – almost the last of his money in the bank – and we said goodbye. I kept looking for his small figure in the ill-fitting uniform long after he had disappeared into the crowd.

The other evacuation ships left that day but the *Duchess of Bedford* was delayed by the bomb damage. Men worked all night making temporary repairs to enable her to get away. Though the bombers came again and again to the docks, she was not hit and at dawn she sailed.

From the deck I watched the island receding. It was the morning the Johore Causeway was blown up and the fight for Singapore was beginning. Against the bright blue sky columns of black smoke were rising above the town. I thought I could pick out the high ground where I had lived at Oxley Rise.

The ship sailed further away till the land became only a bright haze and there was nothing but sea around us.

It was my last sight of the country where I was born.

Chapter Seven

The SS *Duchess of Bedford*, a Canadian Pacific liner in peacetime, had been converted for war purposes to carry six hundred troops. She had arrived in Singapore with reinforcements of Indian soldiers only an hour before we went on board. When she left the following morning with hastily repaired bomb damage in her stern, there were nine hundred women and children sailing with her.

Women were everywhere. Young and old, from different backgrounds, they filled the lounges, they meandered up and down the staircases. Some talked feverishly, some were silent, some were weeping as they watched the island fade into the distance. Children ran round playing their games and seemingly adjusting to their new surroundings. Many women looked dishevelled and few had bothered to put on any make-up, their faces yellow after years or only months of living in the tropics.

They were women in a state of deep distress. The rapid events of the last six weeks had been overwhelming. Only the day before they had parted from the men who belonged to them – husbands, fathers, lovers, friends – not knowing if they would see them again. Their homes were lost and most of their possessions.

They would be considered the fortunate ones who would avoid three and a half years of Japanese internment.

For the Captain and the crew it was a very difficult time. They had been unable to prepare for this great influx of women so soon after the departing troops, unable to clean the ship or get in fresh supplies of food. The repairs to the stern had to be finished properly before the ship sailed very far. The following day the Captain called in at

Batavia, hoping to get the job done there, but the Japs had already landed in Sumatra, and the *Duchess of Bedford* could not stay. After a few hours in port where nobody was allowed ashore, she left, heading for Colombo.

After embarkation, cabins had been allotted by the harassed purser who had worked all day in the heat without ceasing. Those women without a berth – about three hundred of them – had slept the night on the lower decks, bedrolls laid out to mark their sleeping place for the voyage. Buttons and I found ourselves in a small cabin fitted with six bunks. The occupants were all married women, and one had a six month old baby with her. Space was exceedingly limited. Only the bare necessities could be unpacked and were kept on the bunk; the suitcase was then stored in a cupboard.

One of the better moments of those first days of our journey was finding Ricky again. We bumped into her coming down a staircase, and it was good to see her among a crowd of strange faces. It was some time since we had stayed with her and Paddy at their home in Johore. Now he was left in Singapore and she had been parted from him after only four months of marriage.

The worst moment for me happened on the second afternoon. Many of us were lying out on the sundeck when, out of the sky, several planes appeared suddenly, dropping bombs into the sea around the ship. The Jap pilots were clearly visible.

The barking of an anti-aircraft gun positioned nearby roused me from a drowsy state. Over the loudspeaker the Captain's voice ordered everyone to go down to the dining room. Frightened, panicking, clutching life jackets, pushing and shoving, the women poured down the stairways, and all were herded into this small area. Crushed together, it was unbearably hot as we waited, hardly speaking except to bewildered children. If a bomb sank the ship we would die like rats.

An hour passed. The planes did not come back and the Captain's voice was heard again telling us to leave. I had known real fear during that hour – paralysing and degrading. This time there was no exhilaration after danger, no affinity with those who had shared it with me. There was only a sickening dread that it would happen again with worse results.

The *Duchess of Bedford* made slow progress to Ceylon and it was over a week before we arrived. Colombo was full of refugees. Many organisations had already transferred their HQ there to prepare for the next phase of the war. The harbour was full to capacity and so large a ship as ours had to anchor outside. Passengers were allowed ashore, we were told; a launch would go to and fro all day to the quay. After the confinement of the ship it would be a welcome break to walk on dry land again and see other faces for the next few days.

I remember hanging over the deck rail to watch the first launch coming towards the ship. As I looked down on the few people arriving in it, I recognised the familiar bulky figure of Ma.

To find us unexpectedly was the one solace for her in an anguished week.

We had imagined she was sailing to Australia but she had been in Colombo for several days. She told us that after Mark John had left us on the *Duchess of Bedford* he had joined her, and together they had walked the length of the docks to find a boat going to Australia. The last ship they saw was an American destroyer, the *Westpoint*. Women and children were going on board. One of the officers advised them that there would be no more evacuations after that day and suggested Ma sailed with them – the destination could not be revealed – and she could get a ship to Sydney from the next port of call. Poor Ma. Torn between leaving her husband and finding her two young daughters whose whereabouts she did not know, she had to make the decision then. Mark John urged her to leave. He rushed back to the flat and packed a bag for her while she waited at the gangway. The *Westpoint* had intended to sail at 3 p.m. but the planes bombing the docks all day delayed the ship by two hours.

Mark John just got back in time to hand her the suitcase. My parents said goodbye; they had no idea how long it would be before they met again.

The *Westpoint* had sailed swiftly to Colombo. Ma was now staying in the home of a resident, a kind and sympathetic woman. Hearing the *Duchess of Bedford* was moored outside the harbour, Ma had managed to come on the first launch to see us.

Evacuee Committees had been formed in Australia to deal with the many refugees arriving there. Ma had been in touch with Sydney but there had been no news of Pippa and Susan. It was over three weeks since they had left Singapore. Nor had she heard anything of Mark John. She had been going each day to GHQ but could learn nothing. There was talk of mass evacuation of troops, and she hoped he might come to Colombo.

Although the Johore Causeway had been breached, the Japanese had not taken long to land on the northern shore of Singapore and were already shelling the city. Every day they were getting nearer. Every day thousands of British troops, some who had only just arrived on this small island a few days before, were retreating. Lack of air cover was the main reason. The great guns, erected so confidently on the south side of Singapore years before, pointed out to sea and were useless.

The repairs to the damage of the *Duchess of Bedford* took nearly a week to finish. Most of this time we spent with Ma, usually sitting by the swimming pool in the Gaulface Hotel with other refugees. We all talked about the situation and our own experiences. In that twilight time, the final disaster so near, rumours abounded. Mostly they were dispelled as quickly as they started.

I met Major Fisher who was setting up SPRO again, and he wanted me to work in the new office, but by this time, Buttons and I had decided it would be better to go back to Britain and would continue on the *Duchess of Bedford*. Ma was going to wait in Colombo for a reply from Sydney, and in the hope that Mark John might come out of Singapore.

We left on 12th February and the *Duchess of Bedford* started on her long journey round South Africa and northwards through the Atlantic. Once again we said goodbye to our mother, and as usual she told me to look after Buttons. To us she seemed calm and hopeful but really she was lonely and afraid. After so many years of love and devotion to her family, she was unable to be with any of them in this time of stress.

The news of the surrender of the British in Singapore on 15th February came over the ship's broadcast system in the evening of that day. It had been expected. Somehow, though, there had always been hope that a last minute miracle would happen. Now it was final. Now thousands of people on the island – troops, civilians, men, women and children – were prisoners. Few words were spoken after the announcement. For many of the women there were years ahead of sadness and uncertainty.

Life had begun to settle into a kind of routine. The staff tried to run the ship as on a normal voyage. Three meals a day were served at all the separate tables in the dining room which could only hold half of us at a time so there were always two sittings. The catering staff served their reserve supplies – a lot of suet puddings – more appetising in the North Atlantic for which they had been originally provided. No clean napery was possible and the tables collected more and more foodstains. Again Buttons, Ricky and I shared a table as we had done in The Mansion. In spite of the restricted conditions most of us looked clean and tidy and people wore make-up again which improved morale. Not everyone who had bunks slept better than those with bedrolls on the decks. In some cabins bugs had appeared and sufferers scratched their large red bites.

There was little to do except walk around the deck. Women recalled the homes they had abandoned, describing them in minute detail. I felt it was a kind of therapy. I did not hear them talk much about their husbands – it was too difficult to imagine what was happening to them.

Friendships were formed. Quarrels occurred. There was the gossip of the ship – trivia, but it helped to dilute the realities of the situation. A concert was organised by Marie Ney who had been a successful actress on the London stage, and volunteers each did a party piece. It at least broke the monotony of the endless evenings when it seemed as though we had been at sea for months and months.

Our cabin was one of the few free of bedbugs but there was little toleration and much friction over trifles. The other women were older than us. Two of them were wives of civil servants, remaining aloof and not talking much. Another was a regimental sergeant's wife, a real tartar, shouting at the rest of us and insisting on absolute order in the cabin with all possessions tidied away in our bunks. She berated Buttons and me continually and shouted at us if even a shoe stayed on the floor for more than a few seconds. She was fiercely protective of the young mother, a soldier's wife whom she had known before. The baby, aged six months, was a happy distraction for us all, and we cooed over him and tried to help whenever possible.

After a couple of weeks Buttons and I thought we would try sleeping on deck. Two women in a advanced state of pregnancy in whose cabin bugs were rife, were glad to have our bunks. We were glad to be free of the bickering. I heard afterwards that the atmosphere in the cabin was more peaceful after we had gone. Though we did not know it, the pregnant women were officers' wives and the RSM's lady became more subdued.

There was no more room on the lower decks to lay our bedrolls. Every space was occupied. Nobody slept on the sundeck, however, as there was no protection when it rained. We decided to risk it. The following morning brought another disadvantage. Very early, sailors wanting to swab the decks woke us and we had to leap up quickly if we didn't want to be soaked by a strong jet of seawater.

Finally benches screwed to the deck proved our resting place. They were very narrow with curved seats but the hosepipes splashed underneath leaving us high and dry. It was uncomfortable but less oppressive than the cabin, and I liked sleeping in the open air.

There had been several deaths on board since the voyage began. The purser had a heart attack soon after the ship left Batavia, probably brought on by overwork at the embarkation. I heard of two passengers also dying that first week. When the baby in our cabin got pneumonia and died suddenly later in the voyage, it affected us all. I have been to many funerals since then, but have never felt the same sadness as I did when I watched the little coffin slip over the side of the ship and disappear so quickly beneath the waves.

At night I slept fitfully, unable to move much on the narrow curved seat. Lying awake on my back I thought about people left in Singapore. What were they enduring? Throughout my life I had been proud of the British Empire: for several generations since the days of the East India Company my ancestors had helped to build it. In peacetime it had seemed admirable. Yet in wartime it had so quickly failed its subjects. Since I had come out to the Far East life had been wonderful for me. Memories kept recurring, and I did not think I could ever again have the same carefree enjoyment – as indeed I never have. I saw my life ahead as a long unhappy road till the war ended and men were free again.

Restless and uncomfortable I would drift into sleep for short spells, sometimes dreaming that I was with Gerry again in his little MG, driving very fast round the island at night as we used to do. When I woke it was to feel the movement of the ship pushing her way through the Indian Ocean. Above me millions of stars sparkled in the night sky – the same sky under which I had joyously danced on the boat deck of the *Narkunda* less than two years before. From time immemorial those stars had shone down on other human misery besides mine. They had seen the separations of war, the hunger, brutality and death – and would do so many times again. But I did not remember that when I looked up at their glittering canopy.

We seemed to have been at sea for a very long time – it was in fact a month – when I came on deck one morning to find people looking excitedly at the skyline. A faint blur on the horizon could be seen which was becoming larger and more solid as the minutes passed.

The coastline of Africa was in sight.

The first port of call was Durban and it was there that Buttons and I left the *Duchess of Bedford.*

We found out from a War Office official who came on board that, if we wanted to go back to Britain later on, it would be possible for us to do so. Buttons was suffering from painful boils and we both had gastric troubles; the unsuitable diet was probably the cause. We thought it would be a good idea to go and see Aunt Moll in Rhodesia. A cable sent to her brought the brief reply to come.

It was lovely to be on dry land again. Our travellers' cheques, cashed, bought us one-way tickets to Salisbury. Looking at the big map of the African continent in Thomas Cook's office, we found Rhodesia was an area in the middle. Our ignorance of the continent made us surprised to find it would take two and half days to get to Salisbury, including a day's wait in Bulawayo. I had vaguely imagined the journey would be no more than a day.

Other people had left the ship also. Ricky was one of them, deciding to stay in Durban for a while in case there was some news of Paddy. Before getting on the evening train we romped round the town with her, spending most of the residue of the travellers' cheques and ending with a gargantuan meal in Stuttaford's restaurant. We hoped to see her again soon.

Aunt Moll was Ma's elder sister. At different times and in different circumstances the brothers and sisters had gone out to parts of the Empire. Uncle Robin joined the Mounted Police in Canada; my mother – and later her younger sister – were married in Malaya. Aunt Moll and her twin brother, Edward, went to Southern Rhodesia. Aunt Moll, the prettiest sister of them all, Ma told us, had married in Rhodesia. Her father-in-law had played a big part in building railways in the Colony, and had been an associate of Cecil Rhodes. She was now a widow, living with her daughter, Patty, in Salisbury.

This was as much as I really knew about Aunt Moll, but Ma had often talked about their childhood. The family bonds were still close.

As we travelled into Africa towards the plateau that was Rhodesia, I felt glad to be away from the ship but took little interest in this new continent. For hour after hour the next day as we crossed the Transvaal, I saw a bare landscape with occasional boulders and stunted trees relieving the flat expanses. I did not know that historic wars had taken place on this territory. In the last century it had been a setting for battles when British guns and bayonets had defeated the tribesman's spears to make the boundaries of the Empire secure. Later the British had fought the Boers here. For this land much blood had been spilt, and brave men – black and white – had lost their lives. South Africa was an unread chapter in my history book. I really knew nothing of its development.

One thing I did know as the train rattled over hundreds of miles of track: that South Africa was part of the British Empire.

At Johannesburg a sector of shanty towns was our first sight of the city before arriving at the station. There was time for a walk along the main street of skyscrapers and expensive shops before we left again.

A fellow traveller in our compartment pointed out the herds of buffalo drinking at the rivers and we spotted deer running across the plains. Crossing a wide river, he told us it was the Limpopo – a name I knew from the *Just So Stories* – and there were actually crocodiles in the river. Little groups of huts appeared now and then. These African villages were the kraals and the huts were known as rondavels. At the stations which had Dutch sounding names, Africans walked past the carriage window – so dark-skinned and strange after the peoples of the Far East.

Sitting back in my seat I barely glanced at these sights that our passenger was so keen to show us as they passed by. The lush beauty of Malaya was still fresh in my memory. I longed to see, instead, jungle hills and verdant plains, brilliant foliage and water that reflected Asian skies.

A few people got off the train at Bulawayo in the early morning. The Customs Officer marked our suitcases and asked us about ourselves. Hearing that we had come from Singapore, he invited us to spend the day at his home before catching the Salisbury train. His wife put us in her spare room for a rest and we both went to sleep. Waking later in the morning, we found the house full of other housewives. She had invited her friends to meet us and hear about the war in Malaya. Apparently we were the first evacuees to arrive in Southern Rhodesia. I had not thought much about the impact of the surrender on the rest of the world, and I found it difficult to discuss the reason why Singapore fell. Buttons was able to entertain them with her account of our life in the past few weeks.

Many people came to see us off at the station. In Rhodesia it was a custom to greet travellers – and speed the departing ones – whether one knew them or not. The platform was a sea of faces as the train pulled out of Bulawayo.

At Salisbury the following morning there were a great many more people to see us. Local reporters gathered round the carriage wanting to hear our story. We were 'news'. Again I could not say much so Buttons talked to them about her version of events – probably inaccurate, but faithfully recorded in their notebooks.

Suddenly I saw a face in the crowd. It was so like my mother's that I knew it had to be Aunt Moll.

She was with our cousin Patty. Although we had not known them before, we did not feel they were strangers. Aunt Moll had the same blue eyes and soft white hair and the same facial expressions as Ma. Patty was an attractive young woman ten years older than me. Immediately we were glad to be with them.

While we had been crossing the Indian Ocean the situation had changed for our family.

Ma was coming to Salisbury and so were Pippa and Susan. The

Patty.

day after the surrender Aunt Moll had received a cable from Ma
saying that there was now no hope that Mark John would be
evacuated from Singapore, and that she was still trying to get news of
the girls from Sydney.

The day after Ma's cable Aunt Moll got a cable from Pippa and
Susan from a town in Australia called Balaklava. No wonder Sydney
had never heard of them, they had only reached Adelaide before
leaving the ship. It was a worried message saying they did not know
where any of their family were and thought we must all be left behind
in Singapore.

Three cables had then been despatched by Aunt Moll. She sent
one to Thomas Cook in Adelaide instructing them to arrange the
girls' passages to Durban and their journey to Salisbury. She sent one
to Ma persuading her to come straight to Rhodesia. When Thomas
Cook confirmed that the girls would sail, she sent a third to Balaklava
telling Pippa and Susan that Ma and their sisters had got out of

Singapore, and they would be coming to Salisbury when Thomas Cook knew of their sailing date.

Ma was now on the high seas, due to arrive in a week's time. After she had sailed Aunt Moll got our cable from Durban.

Fate and Aunt Moll were bringing the Kennaways on different ships to Southern Rhodesia.

When Ma arrived she was overjoyed to find us here, thinking we must be somewhere in the South Atlantic by now. It was a happy reunion for her and Aunt Moll in spite of the circumstances. The sisters had not seen each other for many years.

Three months later Pippa and Susan's train pulled into Salisbury station. They had been delayed from leaving Adelaide by a long dock strike. Both looked well – much better than expected.

There had been bad times for them, though, since they last saw us.

At first the voyage on the Australian ship *Aurange* with Mrs Payne had been fun. A modern ship, no longer sailing in a war zone, it had been the usual leisurely existence of a peacetime journey. They liked Mrs Payne who treated them as near adults, and they thoroughly enjoyed shipboard life. Spending days on deck in the sun and swimming in the pool was better than going back to a boarding school. They gorged themselves on the large meals in the ornate dining room where the passengers dressed for dinner, the men with their white waistcoats complementing the women's long dresses.

Three weeks' later when the ship called in at Adelaide Mrs Payne's child had become ill. She decided to stay there and take the baby to hospital. An Evacuation Committee took charge of the girls. They were put on a bus and driven thirty miles inland to the small outback town of Balaklava – just one street and a cinema on Saturday nights, they described it later. The old woman with whom they were billeted had not welcomed them. She was old, her house primitive and she had not given them enough to eat. They did not like her peering at them when they undressed, nor did they like the privy at the end of her garden.

The next day Singapore surrendered to the Japanese. Pippa and Susan were in the local Post Office and heard the news over the radio. My sisters, aged thirteen and fourteen, realised suddenly that they were in a country of strangers. They desperately longed to be with their family again.

It was then that they had sent a cable to Aunt Moll.

After several days of the old woman, they decided they would leave the billet at all costs. There was one hotel in Balaklava and, although the money given to them by Mark John was dwindling, they thought they would go there. Here they were lucky. Coincidences are always unexpected. Waiting to see the owner, they had idly looked at photographs of footballers hung on the walls of his office. In one of them they recognised a youthful Mark John. The owner, Joe Burton, remembered him – they had been young men together in Ceylon and had played in the same team. The girls were able to talk to Joe Burton about their father. After that he kept them in his hotel, refusing to take any money, and he and his wife looked after them.

Every day they went in to the Post Office to see if there was a response to their cable, becoming more anxious as the days went by. The reply came at last with the joyous news. Aunt Moll told them that Thomas Cook would let them know when their ship was to arrive in Adelaide. She also sent them money and said Ma would be coming to Rhodesia too.

They celebrated with an orgy of toffees and choc ices, and bought themselves tennis racquets.

Their stay in Balaklava lasted nearly four weeks. During that time the Evacuation Committee billeted them with a family. Here they were not so happy as they had been with the Burtons but eventually Thomas Cook summoned them to Adelaide where they should have sailed immediately. Instead a long dock strike which lasted two months stopped them and they were billeted again in Adelaide, this time with a doctor and his wife. He was an eminent paediatrician and they were cared for with great kindness. Here too they met Mrs

Pippa and Susan at the home of Dr Betts in Adelaide.

Payne again, her child now well. When they finally left Adelaide Pippa's severe acne and boils had almost gone.

On the platform at Salisbury station Ma was waiting for them.

Communications for individual travellers on the high seas were difficult in wartime. With all the chaos of the last days of Singapore, it must have been a nightmare for my mother, her family scattered and she unable to know what had happened to them.

How lucky we all were to have had Aunt Moll. There would have been months of anxiety for us had she not been able to link Ma with her daughters again.

No news came out of Singapore. Nobody knew who was alive or who had died in the past weeks.

Chapter Eight

In 1942 Southern Rhodesia was a British Crown Colony and keenly supported the war effort. Rhodesians were in the armed forces, serving in the colony and in areas of war. Rhodesian servicemen were in Britain, and others were fighting in North Africa, many of them with the King's African Rifles. Several Training Schools for the RAF had been set up in the country, and cadets from all over the Empire were there. Among their instructors were experienced fighter pilots who had fought in the Battle of Britain. In Salisbury a number of women formed the Southern Rhodesia Women's Auxiliary Military Service – known as the WAMS. There were over 160 of these volunteers with two officers, one of whom was our cousin Patty.

Salisbury was a small city in those days with a white population of about 10,000. When I saw it for the first time it reminded me of a set for a Western film. There were Government buildings, but most of the houses were two-storied as were the two hotels which were shabby. The main streets were exceptionally wide, a legacy from the days of Cecil Rhodes when a span of oxen could turn round in them. Jacaranda trees lined some of the avenues. They had recently blossomed when we drove through them that morning, and carpets of blue flowers lay along the verges. There was just one block of flats in Salisbury then – considered very modern – and here Aunt Moll and Patty lived in one of the apartments of this three-storey building.

We had hardly any money and few possessions. Aunt Moll and Patty gave up this flat and found a place where we could all live together.

The house at Cranbourne was seven miles outside the city. Today

Anne and Buttons at Culnagreine.

the city has spread our far beyond this district but then the area was open landscape. Our nearest neighbour was three miles away. Culnagreine had once been a kraal. Set in two acres of ground which had not been cultivated although some trees had been planted, the ten rondavels had been incorporated into the building and were the bedrooms. The space in the middle made an enormous living room as well as a kitchen and a bathroom. Some of these round bedrooms opened on to the living room, others on the edge of the house were entered through the inner bedrooms. At the far end of the garden there was a water tower and a septic tank. Cut into a large rock was a small swimming pool but there was no water and it could not be used. A circular drive led round past the front door and a scarlet poinsettia tree grew in the centre of it. Aunt Moll did not know the people who had once lived here but a row of little gravestones in a corner of the garden showed the names of their departed dogs.

By the standards of those days it was not luxurious but it had a novel charm. I never saw another house like it during our stay in Rhodesia.

It was big enough to accommodate the ménage of Ma and her daughters, Aunt Moll and Patty, and two RAF officers from the nearby Training School who lodged to help with the expenses. The Wing Commander later brought his bride. Friends and relations of Aunt Moll frequently stayed as well. It was always a full house.

The Kennaway family, it was assumed, would remain in Rhodesia until the British returned to Malaya – perhaps before very long. Then we hoped to find Mark John and remake our lives.

Pippa and Susan were sent to school. They had not had any education in the past months and, as there was no school in the vicinity, they had to board. They had become very independent and had enjoyed choosing their own clothes. Susan had bought a particularly hideous dress in Adelaide covered with sequins which Ma thought most unsuitable. They departed reluctantly to Salisbury High School, disgusted at having to wear gym slips and black stockings.

Ma kept house for the assorted household at Culnagreine, alone all day while the rest of us went into Salisbury. Her only help was Isaac, the African houseboy. He had the impressive physique of a Zulu warrior but was, in fact, a most gentle person with a good sense of humour. He and Ma established a rapport. She liked cooking and Isaac was a willing learner, and dinner in the evening was usually a successful event.

Needing to support ourselves and contribute to household expenses, Buttons and I joined the WAMS. Having so few clothes, to be issued with a uniform was a boon. I had little else to wear but the four long evening dresses so hastily packed in Singapore. We were each issued with two khaki skirts, two bush shirts, two pairs of khaki directoire knickers and a forage cap.

I became WA169 Private Kennaway A., and Buttons was WA170 Private Kennaway M.E.

WA Private Kennaway A.

The first four weeks of our army service were spent confined all day in a hot tin hut. This was where we were taught to operate cash registers. The intention was to give each recruit a 'training', making us of use to the Rhodesian war effort. The female dragon who tried to teach us and four others had little patience, and I never mastered these machines. Happily for the Rhodesian Army and for us, neither Buttons nor I were required to touch one again.

Buttons was then assigned to work in Patty's office. Patty was the Adjutant. A charismatic person and a born leader, she had started the WAMS and was the moving spirit of it all. She was boyish looking with a warm personality and a great sense of fun, attractive to men and women alike. Some years before her fiancé had died in a fire on a tobacco plantation and she had not married. We all adored her.

I was posted to King George VI Barracks in Salisbury, the HQ of the Army in Rhodesia. It was a collection of huts erected round a parade ground. In the anteroom next to the Colonel's office I assisted the Orderly Room Sergeant. Beside his work table was a small one for me on which there was a typewriter and a filing cabinet containing details of everyone in the barracks – about six hundred altogether – which I had to keep up to date. Sometimes I typed a letter or took over the barracks switchboard from the WAM operator.

The work was undemanding. I spent a lot of time chain smoking and doing crossword puzzles.

No WAMS were housed in Army quarters. Most of them lived at home. I learnt to salute an officer when I saw one and call him 'sir' – otherwise I was hardly aware of Army discipline. The barracks was a friendly place for the six girls who worked there.

One afternoon a week, though, there was drill on the parade ground for all the WAMS. A bullet-headed regimental sergeant major roared commands at us – 170 women in uniform marching up and down in line. Our uniforms ironed and wearing our directoire knickers, we lifted our knees high as he ordered. From lack of concentration and resenting the whole procedure I – second from the end – was frequently out of step and often the subject of his ungallant comments echoing round the parade ground. Unlike the other women I did not feel it was so important to march as well as the men.

It was good to be living with Aunt Moll and Patty. Aunt Moll was an attractive women in her late fifties, working in Salisbury. There had been sadness in her life but she had remained a happy person.

She and Patty were popular with all their friends and they loved to gather people round them.

Aunt Moll had first gone to Rhodesia at the beginning of the century. Cecil Rhodes had not long been dead and the territory that had taken his name had only recently become British. She and her twin brother, Edward Hick, had come to an undeveloped country. Although railways had been built across wide stretches of land, ox wagons were still a form of transport. As a District Officer Edward had been responsible for a vast area. They had lived in an isolated house, like other African colonial ones, with a red corrugated iron roof and an open verandah all round. There were few amenities and many hazards, and resourcefulness was a necessary quality for survival. I thought it must have been awful to make your own soap out of mealies and to encounter scorpions and other unpleasant creatures, but Aunt Moll had loved the free open air life. A superb horsewoman, she had learnt to shoot the game that roamed in the veldt and had become a crack shot. With an old sewing machine she had made all her own clothes and she was still always well-dressed.

She had been part of Rhodesia's early history and she loved to tell us about it. Once she had gone into dinner on the arm of Rhodesia's Premier, Dr Jamieson, of the ill-fated Jamieson's Raid.

My uncle had been comparatively young when he died. He had been a much-respected District Officer. After his death the Africans in his territory had held a very special ceremony which was rarely held for white men.

By then Aunt Moll had married and had stayed and brought up her children. There had been very few visits to Britain. Rhodesia was her country.

Over the years, as the country developed, it became a pleasant existence for the white Rhodesians. Life was not the great adventure that it had been for the young Aunt Moll. On the tobacco plantations, the cattle ranges and the farms, there were modern comforts and a black labour force more educated than in the early days. In the present white society the first settlers were admired, and stories of their pioneer days recounted with pride.

Reminiscing about their Yorkshire childhood, Ma and Aunt Moll were always talking about their parents and their brothers and sister. Only Robin in Canada was still alive and they had not seen him since before the First World War. The years of separation and the different lives they had led had not changed the two sisters. They joked and squabbled as if they were girls again.

People often called at Culnagreine in the evening for 'sundowners', among them RAF officers and cadets from the nearby Training School. There were not many Rhodesian men as so many were in the Middle East.

There were always a lot of women and I did not find them likable. These young wives sprawled on the large sofas and chairs in the Culnagreine living room, drinking brandy and staying late. They were the daughters of British settlers, born here, and some had never been out of Africa. They were self-assured, capable women, talking earnestly about Rhodesia – about their lives, about personalities in the colony, and the black population whom they appeared to regard with a kind of affection and a certain amount of suspicion. They were in agreement that the blacks had greatly benefited from British rule but there could be no social mixing. The black man's life and culture would not make him acceptable in white men's clubs. That the Government could ever be run by black people was unthinkable.

Proud of their history – Cecil Rhodes was revered – they did not want to live anywhere else but on this beneficent plateau in the middle of Africa. Fervently loyal to the British Empire, with a jingoism of a past era, Rhodesia was referred to constantly as 'God's Own Country'.

I had little contact with the black people except for Isaac. They came into the city during the day and returned to their kraals at night. They seemed a happy friendly people, and I loved to hear them singing as they walked home across the veldt, three or four of them in single file moving in harmony to their rhythmic song.

Restricted by lack of money and wartime conditions, I saw little of the country either. On my army pay I could not afford to travel by train. I was not even eligible for leave for six months. Any journey by car meant a long drive along roads only tarmacked on two strips which went on for hundreds of miles before reaching the next town – and petrol, too, was rationed.

A trip to the Victoria Falls, or to the ancient ruined fortress of Zimbabawe, were not possible in my circumstances. Cecil Rhodes' grave outside Bulawayo high in the Matopa Hills was another sight denied to me.

Most of the time the seven-mile road into Salisbury was all I saw. In my present state of lethargy I did not yearn to go any further.

I made two friends of my own age. They were sisters – Pam and Pat Walker – and we were drawn together by our enjoyment of Noel Coward. Sometimes I stayed the night in their bedsit in Salisbury when we played his records on their gramophone. Pat was a small brunette and was also a WAM. Pam was tall, blonde and beautiful and spoke with a lisp. Young men – and older ones – fell instantly in love with her. I was delighted with them both. They were so friendly, eager to know about the outside world and receptive to my stories. They had been brought up on a farm fifty miles outside Salisbury, and once they took me out for a week-end to stay with their parents – the only time I ever went away from Culnagreine.

I remember the vast outlook, the land visible to far horizons, yet just a pinpoint on the map of Rhodesia. Wild animals bounded among the scrub and drank at the shallow streams. Large birds of prey perched on the occasional thorn trees. At night I heard lions roar. There was no human habitation but this lonely farm. Little had changed in millions of years. I wondered if this was the fascination of Rhodesia so beloved of its white settlers.

Otherwise the days were uneventful. Sundays were spent at Culnagreine, mooching around in the house and talking to anybody who happened to call in. It was not even possible to bathe in the river for fear of getting bilharzia.

Dances were sometimes held in a tin-roofed building known as 'The Club' – at least that was all I ever heard it called. I had lost my enthusiasm for dancing but it was a change to get out of uniform and put on one of the Singapore evening dresses – the only time I ever wore any of them.

Aunt Moll's grandchildren came to stay accompanied by their mother. They were the daughters of her son Billy and lived in Bulawayo. The family were proud that these children were fourth generation white Rhodesians of which there were few in the country. Two little girls played in the garden while the baby was transferred from lap to lap by doting relatives.

Events in King George VI Barracks were the most absorbing for me. I made friends, gossiped, and took an interest in the small dramas that occurred from time to time. I was proud of my meticulously kept records of barrack personnel. The Orderly Room Sergeant and I worked well together. We had both lived in England and we shared jokes and crossword clues. Once I helped him organise a concert. The elderly Colonel, who had retired once but came back to help the war effort, was protective of the WAMS at King George VI Barracks, telling us not to call him 'sir' – just 'Uncle Lawrence'. I even lost my dislike of the RSM who was the epitome of all fearful sergeant majors depicted in cartoons. His whole life had been with the British Army of which he was very proud. When not shouting at us on the parade ground, he was always very courteous and liked to tell stories of his past exploits, interspersed with quotes from *King's Regulations* – always adding the correct number.

The weeks stretched into months. The short Rhodesian winter came when the mornings were crisp and cold as we all piled into Patty's car to go to work. There were often little clouds in the sky but never any rain. June was warm again and by July it was hot. Rain would come later, I was told.

During these months events had gone badly for the Allies in the Far East. The Japanese occupied all of South East Asia and Burma. There was fighting on the frontiers of India. From Singapore there was still no news. There were no lists of prisoners, no accounts of life under the Japs, no letters through the Red Cross. Mark John was presumed to be a prisoner, and Ma now received the half pay of a Captain in the RASC with allowances for Pippa and Susan. This was her only income. She had not been able to get much information on any other financial assets in England. Letters to Britain travelled by sea and took six weeks in transit as did incoming mail. Some never reached their destination – sunk by enemy action en route.

It must have been lonely for her on her own all day, and with time to wonder what lay ahead for us. It was a pity she was not able to meet other Malayan evacuees, but none at this time had come as far as Rhodesia, though there were many in Cape Town and Durban. Her fortitude and the way she ran this large household were admired by everybody.

Of Gerry I heard nothing. I did not know whether he had tried to escape as he said he would, or whether he was dead.

My Singapore days were a long while back. Only the present existed now. The future was seldom more than a week away.

One day there was a letter in the post for me. I was surprised as I had not written any since I had been in Salisbury. Stamped with 'OPENED BY THE CENSOR', the first postmark was a Durban one. It had been addressed to Drummonds Bank in London, our family forwarding address. It had travelled back to Africa again, surviving two wartime voyages through the North and South Atlantic, and reached me in Salisbury after three months in transit. It was from Gerry.

He had written from Durban to say he had escaped from

Singapore, and a month later he had arrived in Ceylon. By then he was ill and the Shell Company had sent him to Durban.

The painful skin condition on his legs from which he had suffered ever since I had known him had at last been diagnosed as a tertiary condition of amoebic dysentery, not detected in Singapore. He was now in hospital undergoing a drastic treatment for this illness. When he recovered he thought he would be sent to the Middle East or possibly to Britain. Assuming that I had gone back on the *Duchess of Bedford*, he hoped we would meet again sooner or later.

Though I was pleased to know Gerry had escaped I did not feel the rapture that might have been if this news had come months ago. During the first weeks in Rhodesia I had looked back so often, remembering the exhilaration of my Singapore days – and the sudden upheaval which had brought grief and disillusionment. Those days would not return and I did not want to think about them any more. It was easier to focus on humdrum life in Salisbury. I did not know how I would feel if I saw Gerry again.

But I wrote back hastily to the hospital address. His next letter was still from Durban. He was sitting on a beach, he said, about to start a month's sick leave. I wrote again suggesting that he spent this time at Culnagreine.

There was a crowd to greet him at the station. After much hearty handshaking with a lot of strangers, we were able to get away and found a bench in the Botanical Gardens where we could be alone. I wanted to know what had happened to him since that last evening in Cairnhill Road when we said goodbye.

On the night before the surrender, Gerry and twenty other Shell employees had escaped in a launch which once used to ferry people to the oil installations on the island of Pulu Bukum. When they had left Collier Quay the city was ablaze and shells were bursting along the waterfront. The launch had moved slowly over the smoke-covered water of the harbour into the darkness and out to sea.

The old craft had taken five days to reach Sumatra, breaking down frequently, and repaired again and again by the engineers on board. Eventually it had been abandoned when it stuck irretrievably on a sandbank some miles up the Indira River. A Pengulu (leader of the village) had met them them at the river mouth. Loyal to the British and dressed impeccably in starched white drill, he had greeted them ceremoniously together with some British officers who had escaped from Singapore in a twelve-foot dinghy. The Shell men were able to join an evacuation order which instructed them to go up river to Rengat where there was a camp and food.

By truck and train, and on foot, the men had crossed Sumatra, not knowing how near or how far away they were to Japanese soldiers. At Padang on the west coast they were able to board a Dutch collier which was about to sail along the coast to Java. Hearing on the Dutch radio that Java, too, was overrun by Japanese, the captain had turned the ship round and set course for Colombo.

Crowded with escapers and with only a small inadequate map produced from somebody's pocket diary, the collier had sailed northward across the Indian Ocean. It had been a journey of long days and long nights, with the constant danger of attack from bombers and the uncertainty that they would ever reach their hoped-for destination. One sardine, a little rice and bread per day was the ration for each man, with restricted cups of milkless tea. Gerry with many others had slept on the coal hatch.

On the ninth evening mountains were sighted – the mountains of Ceylon. The following morning the collier had sailed into Colombo harbour.

Gerry's escape from Singapore had taken twenty-five days. It seemed he had been very lucky. His story was about chance meetings, about split-second timing, and about opportunities seized. All had saved him from death or captivity in a Japanese prison camp. He told me about it very briefly and hardly talked about it much afterwards. But he had kept a diary* which I read later. It was also a story of endurance.

*This manuscript is with the Imperial War Museum.

Sitting among the well-tended shrubs and trees and the orderly paths of the Botanical Gardens, it was difficult to imagine what it had been like. I tried to picture the men on the Shell launch stationary on the open sea between Singapore and Sumatra, dependant on the skill and persistence of the engineers to get them moving again, while Jap planes flew overhead, luckily ignoring them. I thought about the race across Sumatra by whatever means possible in the hurry to leave the island before the enemy took possession, and I tried to picture the mountains of Ceylon as the men saw them after ten days and nights of not knowing where or when they would next find land.

He looked smaller than I remembered and very thin. I hardly knew what to say to him.

If I was shocked by his appearance he was quite dismayed by mine. Over the last months I had become very fat. Rolls of flesh bulged under the khaki uniform. My long blond hair, which he had found attractive, had been chopped short. Strawlike wisps stuck out from under the forage cap. It was not the image of the girl he had thought about during his escape.

He suggested we got married right away.

Luckily we didn't. Neither of us were ready. Instead Gerry stayed three weeks. During this time he grew stronger and regained his buoyant personality. During the day when I was at the barracks he stayed with Ma at Culnagreine. Having seen Mark John after she left Singapore, he was able to reassure her how relieved Mark John had been that we had got away. Ma had always had pangs of guilt that she should have stayed with her husband. Gerry also met the rest of my family of whom he became very fond.

The time went quickly for us. We went for long walks in the countryside around Culnagreine or, if Patty lent us her car, had an occasional evening at Meikles Hotel. Though we made no plans for the future, we were glad to be together again.

At the end of his leave he had to report to the Shell Company in Durban, expecting to be sent to the Middle East or back to Britain. I

Buttons and Gerry.

did not know when I would see him next but we knew we would marry one day.

Again there were lots of people at the station – this time to say goodbye. They all waved vigorously as the train moved away. Gerry was smiling at me through the carriage window and I waved too till he was out of sight. Then I began to weep.

I had not cried since that first morning of the war in SPRO offices when Major Fisher had been angry. Now I couldn't stop. My tears flowed all evening, tactfully ignored by everyone at the long dinner table. I sobbed for most of the night and at last fell asleep among the soaking bedclothes.

When I woke in the morning my mind was clear. Without doubt I knew I must go back to England. In spite of my enjoyment of Malaya and the excitement of Singapore, there had been many times when I had thought of wartime Britain and wished I was there. Suddenly, more than anything, I longed to go back – to see London again and to be among the people with whom I had grown up. The apathy of the past months had gone. I couldn't wait to move again.

I talked to Ma and found she had already considered going back to the UK. Lack of information about Mark John and increasing money worries were making her feel that life would be simpler for her there. It was clear that the war in the Far East would not end for a long while. London would be the best place for her now.

The War Office authorities in Durban granted her request for passages to Britain for her and her four daughters, saying that she must sign a form stating that we travelled at our own risk. We were instructed to go to Durban at the end of September.

There were no difficulties in leaving Rhodesia. As Buttons and I were not Rhodesian citizens it was possible to get a discharge from the WAMs. Nor was it surprising that Pippa and Susan were delighted to leave school again. They had not settled down there and relished the thought of more journeys.

It was from another crowded platform that the Kennaway family and their luggage – old suitcases and some brown paper parcels – got on the train. This time we knew all the people who had collected to say goodbye. Though I had not liked some of them I remembered that they had all welcomed us when we arrived.

I had been in Rhodesia for seven months but I was leaving knowing very little about the colony and its inhabitants due to the restrictions of wartime and my own state of mind. Another time with other circumstances it might have been different.

Saddest of all was parting from Aunt Moll and Patty. They had disrupted their lives when we came, and had tried to make a home for us in the country of which they were so proud. But none of us had wanted to put down roots.

My last memories of Salisbury are of waving hands sending us on our way.

The candle has not burnt brightly in the memory tunnel as I recall our stay in Southern Rhodesia. Little of the landscape appears from the darkness and, except for a few, the faces of people are obscure. Sometimes, though, I have heard voices, and personalities have emerged from the shadows.

It was a place to which I was thankful to come and, during our time there, I was greatly helped to adjust to new circumstances.

I have never wanted to return.

Chapter Nine

Eight days later our ship left Durban. Information on shipping was kept secret, and times and dates of sailing were not known to passengers until the last moment. We had been billeted in a small hotel on the sea front and told that at sometime during the next few days, we would be summoned at short notice and must be ready to sail.

That week had been a happy one. It had felt like a holiday. To see the waves breaking on the shore had been a real delight for me.

We had enjoyed shopping in the big stores, buying clothes for the English winter – especially after I had worn khaki for so long. Except for Ma, who still had the coat she had worn in London before the war, we had no warm clothing. In Britain clothing coupons made a tight rationing system so we bought all we could afford.

Ma had met women she had known in Malaya who had decided to stay in South Africa. Like her they had heard no news of their husbands but she talked over past times with them.

I was able to see Gerry again. He had reported to Shell on his return from Salisbury and was still waiting to go to the Middle East. Then, the day before our boat sailed, he heard he had been seconded to the Admiralty in Durban in the Department of Naval Ordnance. As his illness had left him still in a weakened state, this was probably better for him than the rigours of a war zone.

After all the uncertainty, eventually it was he who stayed in Africa, and I was the one to go to Britain, but the last week had been a bonus for us. We hoped to meet again in London.

*   *   *

The *Orcades*, built in 1936, was the biggest liner of the Orient Line fleet and, with her Master, Captain Fox, she had been carrying troops since the war began. On this voyage there were over a thousand servicemen travelling and a few women passengers. We were the only family in the first class. Mark John's short period of service in the Army entitled us to travel as an officer's family. Among the few women in the second class were a group of nuns and some missionaries.

After the experience of the *Duchess of Bedford* I appreciated the large cabin with six wide berths, no damaged fittings, the blankets new and fleecy and the mattresses uninhabited by other living creatures. A helpful stewardess looked after us. Food was served to a peacetime standard, and the people at our table – some naval officers and an attractive woman travelling by herself – were congenial.

By the time the ship reached Cape Town we had begun to know some of the other passengers. The naval officers had become Bill, Dick and Charles, and were good company. Jean was a pleasure to know. Tall and elegant, with her light brown hair swept up in a coif, I admired her and hoped she would become a friend.

A group of midshipmen were barely older than Pippa and Susan, looking like schoolboys among the other servicemen especially one with a lot of freckles on his face. There were a lively lot and we called them 'Stalky and Co'.

One young Pilot Officer, we noticed, was always nearby. In the saloon or on the deck, by gangways and staircases, he was there – gazing at Buttons but not speaking to her. Perhaps he was too shy, but he was conspicuous with his bright yellow hair and luxuriant moustache. We called him 'The Canary'.

It would be a good voyage, we thought, chattering excitedly among ourselves. We felt optimistic about getting back. Ma talked of renting a small flat in London: she had heard it was possible to work at the Red Cross Headquarters in St James Street, and thought she might hear more news of prisoners in the Far East. Pippa wanted to go back to St Paul's Girls' School where she had been very happy, not having

The Orcades.

cared much for the ones she had been at since, and hoped to sit for a scholarship there. Susan never wanted to go to any school again – she thought all the time about going on the stage and was yearning to go to a drama college. As there was now conscription for girls over eighteen, Buttons and I would have to report at a Labour Exchange within twenty-four hours of arrival in the UK. I hoped I would be able to join the WRNS.

Laughing at our mother as she fussed over us, we intended to enjoy this last interlude before going to the austerity of wartime Britain.

The *Orcades* was not sailing in convoy but I did not feel apprehensive. There was little talk of German submarines and no ships had been lost between Durban and the Cape. As on previous voyages, life boat drill was routine and life belts carried at all times.

Docking in Cape Town, however, Captain Fox learnt that four ships had been sunk in this sea lane during that weekend. It was evident that the area had suddenly become a target for boats. I was aware of greater tension on board.

The stay was short and no passengers went ashore. In the afternoon of 9th October the *Orcades* sailed again.

On deck the sun felt warm as the land receded. Table Mountain rose up to a height of more than 3,500 feet to its table top in a brilliant blue sky, dwarfing the town below. Now that I had read more history of colonial Africa, I knew that Cape Town had begun in the seventeenth century as a staging post for Dutch East India ships round the Cape of Good Hope – once named the Cape of Storms. A colony had grown and had become part of the British Empire in 1815. Many travellers had stopped here. Some had settled with hopes of a new and better life. I looked up at Table Mountain, thinking of those travellers seeing it for the first time after interminable weeks at sea. It must have been unforgettable.

The following morning I woke to find the ship moving swiftly through a heavy swell. Rain was pouring down and the temperature was much lower than on the previous day. Now and then large timbers could be seen in the foaming water. One of the crew told me that the *Orcades* was sailing south eastwards to a stormy area known as the Roaring Forties where it was thought that submarines could not operate.

Feeling thoroughly chilled I had a bath after breakfast, boiling myself salmon pink in hot sea water that gushed unlimited from huge taps. Wearing only a thin blouse and slacks I joined my family in the saloon. It was quiet in there. People were reading or writing letters.

It was then that it happened.

A loud metallic thud from the depths of the ship... the sound of breaking glass... tables falling over. Then a few seconds later another bang.

Everyone knew at once that torpedoes had struck.

Bells began to ring and voices were heard shouting orders. People went on deck to their appointed life boat stations, calm and orderly, obeying all the drill instructions. A bitterly cold wind was blowing and, now cooled from my bath, I was shivering.

I decided to get our coats. Before my mother could stop me I had rushed inside and down the staircases. In the corridor an army officer standing with a revolver asked me what on earth I was doing. I told him, and he came with me to our cabin where I quickly grabbed our coats – our four new ones and Ma's old black one. Looking for something else to salvage, I only saw my eyelash curlers on the dressing table and I seized them as well. During that instant another crash came from below, sounding much louder than the first ones. I felt the ship shudder. At top speed I ran back on deck with a hasty thanks to the officer.

It was probably a foolhardy thing to do, endangering my life and that of the officer, but I was glad we all had warm clothing.

Poor Ma and my sisters had been frantic while I'd been away when the last torpedo was heard. During this time a lifeboat had been lowered and had capsized, spilling out its occupants. They were unable to be saved and the current had carried them away. Among them, we heard later, were the ship's nurse and George, one of the midshipmen.

The order was given to get into our boat and, packed to capacity, it began to descend but was sharply pulled back again. Another lifeboat below had not been able to move away from the ship and we had nearly fallen on top of it. For what seemed like an eternity our boat hovered over the waves, sometimes going up a little, then down again, and then winched up once more. There was a lot of shouting and swearing from the sailors but at last we touched the swirling water. Hundreds of oranges spilling out of the damaged hold floated round us. The men rowed strenuously away from the ship as quickly as they could and out to an alien sea.

Looking down from the deck had not given a real idea of the enormous waves. In a small boat, tossing between them, they were mountainous. Like a roller coaster at a funfair our boat ascended, gliding up and up to the top when – for a brief moment – the whole of the ocean was visible. Above a thin ridge of light on the horizon were massive scudding clouds and the occasional sight of another lifeboat dipping up and down on the foam-flecked waves. Then our boat plunged down again into a threatening valley and we saw only walls of black water till we rose to another crest.

At first it was terrifying. But after many rises and falls I became confident that these boats would not capsize. They were well-designed and the men guiding them were proficient. Some seamen had experienced other sinkings and knew what to do.

The *Orcades* took more than two hours to sink, time enough for everyone to leave her and time enough for Captain Fox to send a message to Cape Town that the passengers were in lifeboats. Now and then across the waves I glimpsed this lovely liner on her side, slowly disappearing into the deep. It was a sad sight.

After the shouting stopped there was an eerie silence. The waves, for all their movement, made little noise. People did not talk much.

The boat was made of steel and held about eighty of us, tightly packed together. I could see Jean sitting between two sailors, still looking elegant with her hair unruffled and her large pearl earrings catching the light. Ma was at one end, Pippa and Susan on either side of her. Her face looked serene as the boat rocked up and down. She had none of the terror that had overcome her during the air raids in Singapore.

Now and then she consoled Susan who kept being seasick. Squashed beside me Buttons sang inappropriate hymns in my ear – she couldn't think of any suitable ones. A seaman in the Merchant Navy told me he had already been sunk six times before in the war. This was a 'gentlemanly sinking', he said, as there had been plenty of time to get away. On previous occasions it had only been minutes before he was in the water. He was a cheerful Cockney and I was glad of his presence.

Although there was talk from the sailors of a naval boat coming to

The Orcades *just after she sank 1942.*

our rescue, we were three hundred miles away from land and it would be unlikely that a ship would appear before two days if they found us. As much as anything, I later realised, the speculations were a way of keeping up morale. When darkness came it would be very cold and more hazardous.

All day long the lifeboats rode the turbulent water. We could not move about and after a time there was almost no conversation. Nightfall drew nearer but the intermittent squalls had stopped and it was possible to see further over the ocean. The other lifeboats had stayed within sight of each other.

I began to be aware of murmurs in the boat. People who had sat still for many hours were twisting round to look at a spot on the horizon.

A ship had been sighted.

Yellow flags were hoisted and flares lit. Would she see our distress signal? If she did... would she come to our aid?

To pick up survivors from lifeboats adrift when a submarine is known to be in the vicinity is an act of bravery for a merchant ship. It endangers the crew for whom the Captain is responsible, and he would not be censured for ignoring the distress signals.

I watched her turn and sail towards us.

Captain Zawada of the Polish steamer *Narvik*, on her way to New York, had heard in Cape Town of the recent sinkings. He had lingered in the area with the hope of saving lives. Spotting the lifeboats, and with the unanimous agreement of his Polish crew, he directed the ship towards the fleet of little boats.

The long rescue began. One by one each boat approached the *Narvik* and was moored to the ship. A large width of coarse netting – known as the scrambles – had been let down against the side. The crew threw down a lifebelt tied to a rope and one by one each person was connected to it, ready to climb up to the deck. Each one was then helped on board by the men above.

Anxiously I watched my mother get ready to go. With her age and weight I wondered if she could make the jump. I had already seen one man fail to catch the netting and be hauled up sharply to stop him slipping into the sea. Luckily, just as Ma was about to leave, a huge wave lifted the boat nearly to the taffrail, and she only had a short way to climb before she was on the ship joining my sisters.

Then it was my turn. With the lifebelt tightly secured round me I waited at the edge of the lifeboat, seeing at close quarters the *Narvik*'s side and the rope netting. I was aware of the rise and fall of the huge waves that slapped against the side of the ship. Deciding my moment I leapt out of the lifeboat where I had sat for many hours and grabbed the scrambles. From then on it was easy. Keeping my eyes on the rope I clambered upwards. Above – though I did not look up – I knew people were waiting to help. As I came to the top I saw a host of faces looking down, hands outstretched to pull me on deck.

The first person I recognised, his hair and moustaches incandescent in the fading light, was The Canary.

The operation continued till the small hours of the morning. Every boat was emptied and every life was saved. This courageous Polish crew picked up over a thousand of us, filling their ship beyond capacity (she normally carried forty-seven seamen). Even her own lifeboats were abandoned to make more room. Had a submarine sighted her then and loosed a torpedo, she would have sunk immediately. There would have been no survivors in that rough sea.

I joined my mother and sisters standing in a passage.

They were unable to sit or move about as more and more of the rescued crowded the *Narvik*. Men edged closer to each other all the time as new boatloads of survivors were taken on board. We were thankful to be out of the lifeboat and sheltered from the winds. Nothing else mattered.

After a while I thought I would look for Jean. I inched my way along the passage, encountering one of the Polish seamen who put his arm around me and suggested I came to his bunk with him. Extricating myself politely I eventually found Jean in the Captain's cabin – a small room which had been made into a sick bay. One of the Polish officers, Stanislaus, was organising the arrangements. Jean, who had worked before in a hospital, was assisting the British Army doctor with the few men who had injuries. Wanting to help, I was allowed to dress the wounds of a seaman who had been badly hurt by an exploding flare. He was very young and in great pain and, though I was a totally inexperienced nurse, he was glad to have someone with him.

Late into the night three men were brought in suffering from utter exhaustion. Their clothes were sodden and their faces bloodless. They looked like ghosts. For several hours they had been in the sea holding on to a raft until they were spotted by people in a lifeboat.

One of them was Captain Fox – the last man to leave the *Orcades* and one of the last to be lifted on to the *Narvik*.

When all the injured had been made comfortable and were sleeping, Stanislaus took Jean and me and the doctor along to his

115

cabin. He was an amusing person with his broken English and his saturnine features. He left us for a short while and came back with a large enamel coffee pot and a plate on which there were three fried eggs. I fell on my egg with joy as I had not eaten since breakfast on the *Orcades* which seemed a very long time ago. We were favoured as it was not possible for the crew to feed all the survivors.

The coffee pot was filled with rough red wine. A celebration followed. Many toasts were drunk – to Britain and to Poland – until the pot was empty.

Then Stan offered his bunk to Jean and me for what was left of the night. Hours in the strong winds, the tensions of the day and the exertions of the evening, as well as an unaccustomed amount of alcohol, overcame my fear of any U Boats lurking beneath the waves. I moved over to make room for Jean and turned my face to the wall. Instantly I was in a deep sleep.

Jean did not sleep so well. She had fought off the attentions of Stan for a long time until he too had fallen asleep. She had tried to wake me, shouting and pummelling, but I had slept through it all, unable to be roused. In the morning we laughed about it, and Stan continued to be as charming as ever.

The day had brought blue skies and a calmer sea. Though there was still a threat from a submarine, it was receding as this overladen steamer made a slow journey back to Cape Town. Men were shoulder to shoulder on deck – cramped, damp and probably hungry, but all good-humoured. The crew had done their best to ease their conditions. There was not much food for this influx of people but all the survivors were given cups of tea.

In the Captain's cabin the patients were better. The seaman whose burns I had tended no longer felt he was dying. He thanked me for my care which pleased me.

My mother and sisters had spent most of the night in the passage until Ma, fearing that Susan who had been seasick all day was suffering from exposure, had found one of the *Narvik* crew.

'American Joe', as Ma called him, had been rather drunk with a bottle of gin sticking out of his pocket, but he and another member of the crew had procured some brandy. He had given his cabin to them. Pippa and Susan had been able to sleep head to tail on the top narrow bunk, Ma and Buttons had taken it in turns with the bottom one.

When I found them they had all recovered and were sitting with the cabin door open, talking to people outside. I quizzed Ma for looking so relaxed instead of worrying over us as she did in lesser mishaps. She didn't mind anything, she said, as long as we were altogether.

Having survived the ordeal we were light-hearted. It was pointless to think about what might happen next. Better to enjoy the sunshine and the breeze that blew less fiercely, and hope that the ship would reach land without further trouble. Some things in retrospect seemed wildly amusing. Bedbugs in American Joe's mattress which had bitten Ma, and my retrieving only my eyelash curlers for the lifeboat were jokes to be included when talking of this adventure in later years.

But our admiration for those sailors who guided the lifeboats over that awesome sea – and for the brave Poles – has never diminished. Always calm and reassuring, they had all sustained us – unprepared and frightened females – throughout the whole experience.

As time went by it got warmer. Later in the afternoon two destroyers appeared. They had been sent by the Navy from Simonstown to escort the *Narvik* for the rest of the journey. When they were spotted there was a loud cheering and the sound of clapping that must have been heard a long way off.

A signal went out from one of the destroyers as they got close to us. Was there anything needed on board? The answer went back – the *Narvik* had run out of tea. It was too rough for any boat to row over to her but a line was shot over her bows, landing on deck, and supplies of tea were slung along it. Copious cups of tea were again given to everyone – a lot had been drunk in the last two days.

Soon the sinking of the *Orcades* and the rescue of her survivors by the *Narvik* crew would become just another story in the records of war at sea.

The ship reached Cape Town early next morning. Once again I approached the shores of Africa, and for the second time in three days I looked up at Table Mountain – yet another traveller glad to see this impressive sight after a long while at sea. Far below it Cape Town lay before us.

As the *Narvik* sailed into the harbour there was a Service of Thanksgiving on deck. Everybody who could attend was there, crushed beside each other wherever there was room. The engines had been switched off and, as the steamer glided silently across the still water, the words of the padre reached every corner of this memorable ship.

While the men disembarked Captain Zawada stood on the bridge watching them. Hundreds of soldiers, sailors and airmen were going down the gangway in single file. Jean and I went up to thank him for our rescue. He spoke no English but we shook hands. Words were inadequate anyway.

Chapter Ten

A grand reception awaited our arrival. High ranking officers – brass hats from all the Services – stood on the quayside. There were also Cape Town dignitaries and ladies from welfare organisations. A larger woman dressed entirely in purple stepped forward and spoke to Ma, saying she felt sure we were all longing for a cup of tea.

In a canteen everybody sat down to a three-course meal. It was wonderful to see food again and I ate heartily, realising how hungry I was.

The euphoria that had existed on the *Narvik* now began to ebb away. Like others, I felt tired and dirty. We smelt of stale sweat and our clothes were still slightly damp.

After the meal the survivors of the *Orcades* and the crew of the *Narvik* dispersed. Brought together for an intense forty-eight hours we would not meet again. The Servicemen went to Army, Navy and Air Force bases, the Polish seamen back to their ship, and the staff of the *Orcades* to the care of the Orient Line. No doubt the nuns were looked after by their religious order.

The Kennaway family, Jean and a few other women were taken by Lieutenant Martin, the Services Families Officer, to the Grand Hotel in the seaside suburb of Muizenburg. It had not yet opened for the summer season and we were billeted there. We all fell into beds provided and I remember I slept till the following morning.

The next day one of the welfare ladies called at the hotel. She was from the committee of 'Bundles for Britain' – a charity which had been collecting clothes for bombed-out people in the UK. We were taken to a large warehouse which was stacked with donated clothes. Coats, dresses, suits for men and women hung in rows. Shelves were filled with underwear, blouses, skirts, jerseys, shirts as well as hats and handbags. Everything that someone in our situation might need was there. All were in good condition – there was nothing shabby or well-worn. Some members of the Committee were sorting garments and making them into bundles to be sent to the UK. From this surplus of the charity's store, we were invited to choose what we would like. To have had a bath and to wear clean clothes again helped us all to regain a feeling of normality.

Later in the day Lieutenant Martin came to the hotel. He told us that it was hoped to send us on another ship very soon. Until then we would stay here.

The following days were spent sitting on the beach watching the waves that lapped gently on the sand. The white houses of Muizenburg with the jagged ridge of mountains so close behind – and the warmth of the sun – reminded Ma of the French Riviera.

If she felt dismayed by the latest mishap to her family she did not appear to show it. Losing all our possessions did not seem to matter much at this time. We kept remembering valued things that had gone down with the *Orcades*. Susan mourned the loss of her diary which she had written since she was a child. But my long evening dresses which had filled my suitcase when leaving Singapore had not been of much use since and I did not really regret them: no – not even the oyster satin I had once loved so much. In my handbag I had a lipstick, powder compact and comb – also the eyelash curlers. I had, too, some letters from Gerry and my passport. Ma's capacious reticule held her spectacles, useful addresses she had jotted down, recipes for meals she intended to try one day, letters from friends and various knitting needles and patterns. Hardly any money though – just a ten shilling note in her purse. The money for the journey and the other passports had been stored in a suitcase under the bunk.

I wrote to Gerry in Durban to tell him what had happened. He

120

already knew. His job in the Admiralty had allowed him into the Operations Room and he had been there when the *Orcades* was hit. He had heard the message coming through that the passengers had taken to the lifeboats.

Was it a good idea to go? he wrote back. It might be better to stay in Cape Town now and as soon as he could get leave he would come and see me. But I still felt committed to getting back to Britain – as Ma did – and this he understood. We longed to be together again but he was not due for leave and I could not leave Cape Town in case our ship came. We could only communicate by letters.

Mr Martin came again at the end of the week to say that there were no berths for us yet but we would sail before the end of the month. A rather shy young man, we thought, not used to dealing with women. He told us he had been a tea planter in Assam before the war and had joined the Army expecting to be sent to the Middle East. A bout of fever had made him unfit for active service and he had been assigned to the Services Families Association dealing with their welfare.

Bill and Dick, the naval officers at our table on the *Orcades*, came over from Simonstown and sat on the beach with us. Stalky and the other midshipmen also came, sad in their silent way about the death of George who had been in the capsized lifeboat. They were suddenly older – no longer the boys who had joked with Pippa and Susan a week before.

Since 1910 when the Union of South Africa was formed, Cape Province was one of the four states. Centuries of history when African, Dutch, British, Malay and others had made their home here, made Cape Town an interesting city. Though there was a section of Afrikaners with memories of the Boer War who were pro-German, most people we met were whole-hearted in their support of the British. Men and women had joined the Forces, and flag days for war charities were well-subscribed. The Prime Minister, General Smuts – a Boer veteran – was a liberal and highly respected by the Allied leaders. His wife was a popular figure, known affectionately as 'Oma', the Afrikaans word for grandmother.

There was a lot of hospitality offered to servicemen stationed in the country, and to the men who came off the troopships which stopped for a few days on their way to India, others going homewards or to the Middle East. On these occasions the town was suddenly full. Troops wandered aimlessly in the streets until they were collected and welcomed into Cape Town homes. As no ships had been sunk in this area before, civilians in our situation were uncommon. People wanting to help sent clothes to the hotel. Among them was a parcel from Mrs Hertzog, the wife of an anti-British Minister in the Government. On hearing that Ma was stout like herself, she had thoughtfully sent some of her clothes which might fit – among them a blouse made of loosely knitted string with a large frill hanging down in front which reminded us of the scrambles. The bonds of fat women are stronger than politics, we joked with Ma. The blouse did not suit her, but she wore it with her natural dignity in spite of our laughter.

Three weeks had now passed since we landed here. Our naval friends had sailed and even Jean was staying with a new friend. This life in limbo was becoming tedious.

It was even more frustrating for me when the victory at El Alamein made the headlines. After three years of fighting this was the first major success for the Allies, and all over the world those who supported them rejoiced. The reoccupation of Europe was a step nearer. In the streets of Cape Town the people greeted each other excitedly – there were many South African men in the Western Desert. More than ever I longed to be in Britain.

Soon after this Lt. Martin called again. He explained there was a setback for us. Since the weekend when the *Orcades* was sunk,* many more ships had been lost between Durban and Cape Town. Other

*It was later discovered that the Assistant Harbour Master in Cape Town was a Nazi agent and had been responsible for the sudden increase of sinkings including the *Orcades*.

people were waiting to sail and, with a major offensive in the Middle East, all berths had been commandeered. Our priority was low on the list. Though we must always be ready to sail at a moment's notice, he thought it might be two months before our turn came. In the circumstances the Army would cease paying for our accommodation. The Grand Hotel was ready to open for the summer season and wanted us to leave.

This was a blow. I was bitterly disappointed and, although she did not say anything to Mr Martin, Ma was worried as she did not know how far her money would stretch. To live on her Army allowance (Mark John's half income), which was now being paid into a Cape Town bank, would be very stringent. A sudden drastic change in her financial situation had happened before in Ma's life – more than once – and now it was happening again. So far our losses from the war in Malaya had been a lesser worry than not having news of her husband – she had felt she could cope once we were in Britain. But now she realised this new circumstance would be harsh.

Ignorant of how to go about it, I began to look for a job. My previous ones had been easy to get so I was optimistic. Wearing my Bundles for Britain outfit I started early in the morning of the following day at the bottom of Adderly Street, the main centre of Cape Town, going into shops and offices asking if they needed a temporary secretary. I explained that I might have to leave without notice as I was waiting for a ship.

Sometimes my reception was polite. Most times it was a monosyllabic refusal. Nobody wanted a secretary who might go at any moment.

By mid-afternoon I had reached the top of Adderly Street without success. Tired and disconsolate, I sat on a seat near the Mount Nelson Hotel – a large Victorian edifice from Cape Town's colonial past – and wondered if it was worth going on. How stupid I had been to think I would get a job in this way. I began to be fearful about the future. Today I would carry on; tomorrow I would go about it

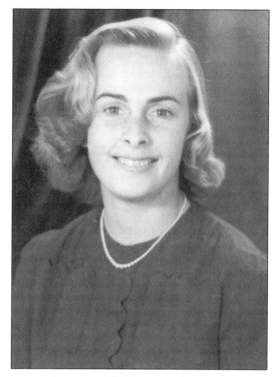

Anne – an OK Bazaar photograph.

differently. Perhaps I could find somebody who knew my situation and let me do some work for them.

Moving again I passed a cul-de-sac and saw a tall modern building at the end of it. This skyscraper was the office of the Shell Company and I went inside.

In the entrance hall the clerk at the Reception desk gave the same response as the other offices that morning. Turning to go away I remembered an incident on my last chaotic day in Singapore. Meeting for a brief moment a man I knew slightly and telling him I was leaving, he had offered to write a letter of introduction to his friend in the Shell Company in Cape Town. I had accepted with no particular thought of ever using it. This letter had been lost with my other possessions in the *Orcades*, but I could remember the name on the envelope. It was addressed to 'Mr Webster'.

The clerk looked surprised when I mentioned this name and asked me to wait. After a telephone call I was escorted in the lift up to the top floor and met by a pleasant middle-aged secretary. A few minutes later she had taken me into a spacious carpeted room where Mr Webster sat at his desk. I had not known that, as well as being General Manager of Shell in Cape Town, he was also the head of all the Shell Companies in the southern half of Africa.

After a morning of rejections it was wonderful to find him so friendly. When we talked about the writer of the letter who was still in Singapore, I explained why I no longer had his letter and how – due to the delay in sailing – I needed to earn some money.

My search for a job ended then. I could work in the typing pool, Mr Webster said, and when I pushed my luck further and told him I had a sister who needed a job too although she couldn't type, Buttons was included as well. We could both start the following Monday.

Now that we knew how much money we would earn – my salary was three pounds a week with a six shilling living allowance – Buttons and I looked for somewhere to stay. Near the Shell Office we found The Gardens – a small boarding house which we thought would do. But I looked at the poky bedroom with distaste. Between the two beds an ugly dressing table blocked the light and the view of the garden. Along the passage the ancient geyser in the bathroom exploded when I lit it, and grit continued to fall in the slow stream of water as I ran a bath.

We agreed it was depressing but at least we were independent of Ma.

All day Ma had looked at boarding houses which she felt she could afford. Eventually the decision was made between The Oaks and The Haslemere. Their names may have echoed a rural England but there was little in either of them to remind us of a green and pleasant land. The Oaks was the cheapest, and Ma and the girls had moved in there.

After the comforts of the Grand Hotel this place looked rough. It was a terraced house in a street near the docks, and the rooms were small and meagrely furnished. Pippa and Susan's room was inside the house, but Ma's was outside in the back yard – a dark cell with one little window.

I queried Ma's choice. Surely there was something better than this? It was awful. She said she could manage if she and the girls stayed here. After all, it was only for a short time. Before long we would be on a ship again.

Once I had accepted I could not leave Cape Town immediately, there was much to enjoy.

The summer had started and the sun shone all the time. The Cape Peninsula, with the extraordinary ridge of Table Mountain high above, had green valleys below and a varied coastline with sandy bays and rocky cliffs. Flowers and fruit were abundant and cost little. The people who passed me in the streets – black and white – were lively and colourful.

There were different beaches where I bathed and I found good walks to explore. Jean and I liked the Constantia Valley, strolling along the paths between slopes where vines were planted. Stalls by the wayside sold succulent grapes the size of plums. These could not be exported as they had once been in peacetime, and we bought them for 3*d.* a bunch, popping them in our mouths as we went along.

A longer expedition was the climb to the top of Table Mountain. There the southern coast of Africa lay below us. One view looked on a sandy sea and beyond the Indian Ocean from where we had come. Another view from the Mountain looked westwards at waves breaking against rocks – the Atlantic, over which one day we hoped to sail.

With easy access to a library I read history books and got through a great many novels. To be able to gaze into shop windows again was a pleasure even if I couldn't afford to buy much but the OK Bazaar was a godsend, selling a varied assortment of cheap goods.

Our boarding house wasn't so bad. The pretty garden was a good place to sit with a book and with my usual excellent appetite I was not critical of the food.

In the Shell Building the typing pool was a large room on one of the higher floors and had big windows on two sides. Desks placed in twos by these windows so that the girls faced each other as they worked made a friendly atmosphere. Enthroned inside a glass partition sat the head typist with the telephone on her desk. Each girl worked for a special man and he rang the head typist when he wanted his secretary. I did not work for anyone in particular but I typed invoices and big sheets of figures – and enjoyed the view of Cape Town roofs from my bit of window.

In between the typing the talk was mostly about men. I learnt about the bosses, and about the girl's fiancés – I heard who was fighting in the Western Desert and who was engaged and who was married. Joining in the chatter I was glad to keep my typing skills in practice.

Every week I went to the cinema. In Cape Town they were called 'bioscopes'. At the back of each seat there was a ledge where a tea tray could be served to the person sitting behind. *Dangerous Moonlight* was a film about the blitz in which the hero – a pianist from war-ravaged Poland – played the Warsaw Concerto while German bombers flew over London and burning buildings crashed around him. The heroine, a cool English blonde, stood listening. Now she too could share his suffering.

I sat in the dark looking up at the screen and munching cake – and wished with all my heart that I could have been there.

Money was tight for Ma but she met people who were helpful. Pippa was able to get an office job in an insurance firm. She was now fifteen and could legally work – and she was very pleased with her pay of 7*s.* a week. With her intelligence and her bright face she was probably an asset. Susan went to a typing class where the instructor, on hearing of her wartime circumstances, waived the fees. She practised hard and dreamed of the time when she could go to RADA. To get some pocket money she did our washing. For a charge of 2*d.* or 3*d.* a garment, 'Susie's Steam Laundry' returned her sisters' clothes washed and ironed.

It was the people we met who made our stay there so much more enjoyable than it might have been. Hospitable and kind, they asked us to their houses and to the parties and dances which they frequently gave for the Forces. I now had two dresses to wear on these occasions. One was a short black one with a frilly lace collar and cuffs which I had bought, the other a long pale blue crepe cut on Grecian lines which somebody had given me and which fitted quite well.

It was a pleasant life really, but at any time we expected to go at twenty-four hours notice. A telephone call from Mr Martin and we would leave it all behind.

The Empire Club was a boon for Ma. It was a room in a building near Adderly Street, furnished with comfortable chairs and where there was a lunch counter. She spent much of the day there, often helping at this counter which was run on a voluntary basis. I found her here when I came in for crayfish sandwiches which I remember were particularly good. A lot of women congregated at this club which was a place where women from other parts of the Empire could meet Cape Town residents. Ma talked to evacuees from Malaya and they exchanged gleanings of news but there was really no information coming from the Japanese. The women reassured each other that their husbands would surely be treated well according to the rules of the Geneva Convention.

It was through the Empire Club that we had our first report of Mark John. Christmas had come and gone but a few days afterwards a club member, a South African, listening to her short wave radio, heard a broadcast coming from Japan. Some names of British prisoners of war were being announced. She thought she heard our father's name among them and she quickly passed this news to Ma. There were no other names she recognised – and she wasn't absolutely sure if it was Mark John's name she had heard.

At least there was hope that he was alive. Somewhere, on the other side of the world, he was there. One day we might see him again. So many thoughts came crowding back to us. It seemed more urgent than ever to go back to Britain. Ma spoke regularly on the telephone to Mr Martin but, although it was more than two months since he had told us of the delay, there was still no prospect of a ship.

The days began to drag by. Each morning I woke hoping that this would be the day we would pack our bags and go on board. Sometimes I felt I could not bear to wait another day longer.

January was a hot month. It was too hot. Often a thick white cloud hid the top of Table Mountain, which the townspeople called the 'Tablecloth'. A 'southeaster', the strong wind that blows in from the sea for several days at a time, sent up swirls of dust in the streets and made my mouth feel gritty as I walked down the hill.

Ma was becoming very irritable, I noticed. Pippa and Susan said The Oaks was more horrible than ever these days. The boredom, the cramped space and the heat made them all bad-tempered. They had discovered The Oak was a hostel for seamen; sailors came in and out but they saw little of them. The landlady was not welcoming, even hostile to Ma, and they seldom saw her either.

I hardly ever went to The Oaks. The Empire Club was an easier place to see my family than to walk the extra distance through unprepossessing streets to this hostel. One afternoon I did walk down and found my mother sitting on a wooden chair in the yard. She was sewing. Lately she had started making dresses for us – a slow and eye-straining business without a sewing machine. She was very gloomy when I talked to her, wondering how much longer we would be in Cape Town and fearful for our future in years to come. I had not seen her so downcast before. At the Empire Club or anywhere else she was always cheerful and liked by everyone.

It was airless in that yard. No bush or tree relieved this enclosed area, and the harsh sunlight exposed the dirt in its corners and crevices. A smell of stale food permeated the place. The outside lavatory with its unvarnished wood seat and cut-up squares of newspaper was at least clean. In Ma's dark bedroom I saw the narrow bed and her clothes hanging on a row of nails in the wall. Below them a pair of shoes on the floor had been a gift from Mrs Hertzog. They had not fitted and mice had tried to make a nest in them.

Noticing how lined her face had become, I realised that the strains of the past year and the long wait in this squalid place were taking their toll. At that moment I was acutely aware of her unhappiness.

Anger welled up in me. Things should not have come to this. The anger was fuelled by guilt that, absorbed in my own affairs, I had not bothered much about Ma's welfare. I took for granted her capacity to cope with trouble whatever it might be.

Rushing round to Mr Martin's office, I poured out my feelings. This quiet young man, our link with Army Transport, had always been understanding whenever Ma had telephoned or gone to see him. He had not known until I told him how little money she had, assuming that she had other funds beside her Army allowance. Getting up from his desk he came immediately with me to The Oaks. He appeared shocked when he saw the place and Ma, now rallied from her despondent mood, sat him on her chair and poured him a whisky, while he repeated emphatically that she and the girls could not remain there.

On his report the Army authorities decided to accommodate us again till they could put us on a ship. Before the end of the month my mother and sisters had left The Oaks.

The Kingsfold Residential Hotel was in a quiet leafy street near the Cathedral. A solid house surrounded by a garden, it was run by three sisters – the Miss Wilsons. It was comfortable and the Miss Wilsons were anxious to do all they could for Ma. Her money worries were eased for the time being. The guests were mostly old ladies, forever waiting – it seemed to me – for the dinner gong to sound. Not surprising as the meals were delicious. Ma, Pippa and Susan were delighted to be there.

Buttons and I were pleased with our move too. The Army billeted us in a private house out in Wynberg. This suburb had wide roads with large old houses where flowering trees hung over garden walls. It was a tranquil part of the province near Constantia and had been the centre of wine making for more than a century. Each day we took the train into Cape Town – a half hour journey travelling through other suburbs. Public notices were always printed twice, first in English then in Afrikaans. *'All stasie naar Kapstadt'* was the only Afrikaans phrase I ever learned.

Rosalie, our hostess, was a cultured woman in her thirties, tall and lean with beautiful dark eyes, and her husband was a physician with a consulting room in Cape Town who came home at weekends. She and her two children made us feel welcome, and we loved the large double-fronted house with wide sash windows and the garden full of Cape flowers.

Her friend Polly, living near, gave exciting parties which occurred frequently. She had come out from England with her son and friend who were music students, for the duration of the war. Barely five feet tall, her luxuriant red hair twisted in a coil on top of her head, Polly was a singer with the temperament associated with opera. Though I never heard her sing on the stage, I was told her voice had huge strength for her small form. Musicians and others connected with the Arts gathered at her house, playing impromptu music and talking late into the night. I was unused to the informality of these parties and, as I sat on the floor with a glass of wine, I enjoyed listening and observing these talented people.

A frequent guest was Dr Pickerell, a white-haired extrovert who was the conductor of the Cape Town Municipal Orchestra. His

Promenade Concerts on Sunday evenings were very popular. Over the months I widened my appreciation of good music. The opening chords of Tchaikowsky's First Piano Concerto, played so often at that time, will always bring a memory of soldiers, sailors and airmen together with Cape Town enthusiasts queuing outside the Concert Hall to fill the auditorium each week.

After six weeks at Wynburg, Buttons and I were moved to the Kingsfold as the likelihood of our sailing was probable, Mr Martin told us. We said goodbye to Rosalie. How much she enjoyed having two boisterous girls staying with her, I do not know, but as for us it was quite the best part of our stay in Cape Town.

A few days later the call came. On Friday we were told to be ready by the week-end. I collected my pay from the Shell office, said farewell to many friends, and wrote a hasty letter to Gerry, discreetly worded to pass the censor. Excitedly we packed our suitcases bought in readiness from the OK Bazaar months before.

On Sunday a troopship left Cape Town, taking Jean and others we knew but – after all – not the Kennaways. Perhaps there had not been room for a large family. We were not told the reason. It was disheartening after the anticipation, but we became resigned to waiting once again.

On Monday morning I was back in the typing pool.

My twenty-first birthday came a week later. It was celebrated with my family at the Kingsfold. Ma bought a bottle of sherry and we took our toothmugs to her bedroom where she and my sisters drank my health. They gave me their presents – flowers from Susan, ear rings from Pippa which she had made herself, and a red bag from Buttons to match a dress from Ma. It was not the riotous party I had once intended to have at Escot. We wondered what Mark John was doing and whether he had remembered the day.

Afterwards, wearing my new red dress, I went on to a party – like many I had been to over the months. A troopship had arrived and some of the soldiers on it had been brought to a Cape Town home for their short stay. There was plenty of food and drink in the room full of cigarette smoke. I remember I talked to a young officer, asking him about Britain and about his war experiences. We exchanged our short life histories and he showed me a recent wedding photograph. He was in uniform and his bride wore a plain suit. Few brides could spare clothing coupons for an impractical white dress, but her extravagant hat, wide brimmed and trimmed with veiling, was coupon free. Dark eyed and slender, she looked very happy. I did not see him again after that evening – this was a brief interlude before the men left next day for war in the jungles of Burma. I hope he was reunited with her eventually.

At last. In April another summons came. Within hours we were aboard, parting from Mr Martin who is still remembered with affection. The *Stratheden* sailed the following morning.

The Cape is one of the beautiful places in the world, and we were lucky to have landed there. We left its riches for wartime Britain – for the austerity of rationing, conscription of labour, its battered cities and the probability of more air raids. But Britain was where we belonged now.

Chapter Eleven

$\mathcal{I}$ was at sea again. My journeys on ships over the past three years had been so different, each with experiences unlike the others.

This one was different too. The *Stratheden* travelled with a convoy. She and the *Duchess of Devonshire* were both carrying troops as well as women and children, having started the journey in India. A Royal Navy destroyer accompanied them. It was reassuring to see this smaller vessel dipping up and down on the waves between the two liners.

One morning, soon after the voyage began, there was an alert. At the sound of the alarm bell people rushed to their lifeboat stations. But I could not move. I was rigid with a sick fear – thinking of an open boat tossed by enormous waves and feeling sure that we would not survive a second time. A memsahib pushing past shouted at my cowardice as I hindered her passage but, unable to speak, I could only flash her a contemptuous look. What did she know of the horrors of the open sea? After a minute my terror subsided and I too could join the stream of hurrying people.

A false alarm was announced soon afterwards. I felt very shocked at my reaction which I had not expected. So strong had been my desire over the past months to get to England, I had hardly paused to imagine another submarine, another lifeboat and more hours, days and nights adrift.

After this incident I constantly aware of this possibility and was more nervous than I had been on other journeys in spite of the destroyer always in sight.

There were no more alerts and there was little to remember about the voyage afterwards, which took three weeks with a day's stop at Freetown. The *Stratheden* was an old P&O liner and had done much service. She was now full to her wartime capacity. I shared a small inside cabin with Henrietta, a young wife whose husband like my father was a prisoner of war in Singapore. It was dark and windowless, and unknown insects crawled out of the woodwork and bit us while we slept. The days were long and the nights uncomfortable. We all wanted the time to go quickly.

But, as on other voyages, I could lie in my bunk at night, listening to the muffled noise of the engines, the creaking of the ship's timbers, and feel the rocking motion which could send me to sleep. When the days were sunny I could still stand by the deck rail, enjoying the breeze on my face, and see the ever moving surface of the ocean and the clouds above that faraway line where sea meets sky. I could look down again at the waves surging round the ship, see the light on the surf and the mysterious darkness of the water below.

This was a delight and would be always.

As we sailed northwards the sea became rough and the hot enervating weather changed to stormy conditions. I expended a lot of pent-up energy walking round and round the deck, Atlantic winds tearing at the roots of my hair, and wondering what my immediate future would be.

It was the right decision to return to the UK. We did not regret it. We came back to a country where war was now a way of life. People were united by a common bond – the will to win. Class distinctions muted, rich and poor restricted by shortages, families separated and loved ones lost, they shared the same hardships.

These were my impressions when I first came back. It seemed a better country than the Britain I had left behind.

Ma was able to work at the Red Cross Headquarters as she had wished, and soon after our return she rented a flat. No. 8 Kings Mansions was on the top floor of a red brick block near the Chelsea

Embankment. Four flights of stone steps led up to it and, behind the front door, three rooms, a kitchen and a bathroom opened off a short passage. The small sitting room was square with a window that looked down on the street and on to the roofs of Peabody Buildings opposite. An old gas fire spluttered in a comforting way when lit and, furnished from the old Holland Park house, the room had a familiar feeling with the sofa and armchairs covered in Ma's hollyhock chintz and the railway posters of summer scenes on the walls. The kitchen, bathroom and box bedroom looked down on the well between the two blocks of flats, but Ma's room at the end of the passage had a view of the Thames as it flowed past Lots Power Station and under Albert Bridge – rather beautiful on a misty morning.

The flat was too small for her needs. There was always one of us sleeping on the divan in the sitting room, and others, friends and relations, often came there. But with our lives going in different directions, we were glad to have a base again after being so long without a home.

Pippa and Susan lived there at first. Had it been possible Pippa should have continued to higher education but there was not enough money. Instead she worked in a library until at eighteen she joined the WRNS. Susan still had to endure another year at school before she could go to a drama college and start her longed-for stage career.

Buttons was drafted into the WAAF and was eventually posted to Egypt. I was sent to SOE Headquarters in Baker Street where I worked in the Danish Section, spending the summer in Denmark after the Danes' liberation. I lived in London for the rest of the war and a long time afterwards.

On this candlelight journey I have seen my emergence from a cocooned adolescent into the upheavals of a war – the stark horrors of which I came so near but never really experienced. Much could have happened to leave lasting sorrow, but I am thankful that this story has a happy ending.

I never went back to any of the countries mentioned in these pages. I have not sailed across Cape Town Harbour and seen Table Mountain once more, towering above the Bay, and the sunshine on that sapphire sea that surrounds its shores. Nor have I known the awe of a night in the veldt under the African stars. I have never returned to Singapore to walk along the slopes of Oxley Rise or danced again at Raffles Hotel. Old haunts – if they have not been demolished – would be difficult to find among the tower blocks. Flame-of-the-forest trees still flower on the jungle hillsides of Malaysia but I have not been back to the country of my beginning.

So many people I knew during that time I have never met since. The war severed many friendships. Those that are still alive will now be old, and it is likely I would not recognise them today. But the candlelight shines on them as they looked over fifty years ago and I have enjoyed knowing them again.

I have been glad that I saw something of the British Empire – the good and the bad – before the established order changed and its story went into the history books.

A year after we came back to Britain – that summer after the Normandy landings when Allied troops were pushing across Europe and liberating the occupied countries; the summer when in London and the South East, pilotless planes and V2 rockets were dropping bombs, and we were learning to cope with a new kind of air raid – Gerry came home.

At that time I was sharing a flat with Henrietta at the top of a tall house in the Kings Road; empty floors were below and a bakery at street level. One evening I heard the door bell ring. It had been a long day and I stumped rather crossly down the four flights of steep stairs to find him on the doorstep.

It was certainly a surprise. I had not known he had left Durban. His last letter, written before he sailed, had not arrived.

He had some leave before he was posted to the north of England, and we spent it together in London. It was a different city from the one we had talked of when we first met in Singapore but we decided that London was where we would live when we married.

Three months after the end of the war with Japan, Mark John returned. He was then sixty-five and had been for nearly four years a prisoner-of-war in Changi Camp on Singapore island. I first saw him again in a military hospital. He was frail and emaciated and had survived a major operation performed during his internment but he was unchanged from the loving father we had always known. He and Ma lived at Kings Mansions until he was well enough to return to Tanjong Malim seven months later and start again at Escot Estate. The bungalow was totally despoiled and inhabited by rats. But Hi Ho and many others from the village were there to give them a warm welcome.

In 1950 the estate was sold. The old bungalow was demolished and a modern stone one built somewhere else on the estate. Probably there is not a trace of our old home among the rubber trees that must be covering the site.

For the next few years Mark John worked on rubber estates, building up his finances. Sometimes the jobs were dangerous for planters during the Communist Emergency but they were well-paid and he was able to retire with a comfortable income. He left Malaya for good in 1957 – with sadness for he had loved the country for nearly sixty years.

Mark John and Dorothy's last home was on a high ridge below which lay the Kent countryside. In winter the winds from the east howled round the house but in springtime the orchards were white with blossom and new-born lambs frolicked in the lush green grass. As at Escot their house was often filled with family and friends and every school holidays their several grandchildren came, and it, too, was a special place for them. After all the diversities of their past life together, their few remaining years were serene.

My parents died within a year of each other – they were courageous people.

Wedding, 4th March 1946.

The wedding party.

The immediate post war period was austere. The transfer to a more affluent way of life took several years. People returning from overseas found housing shortages, rationing still in force, and not many goods in the shops while industry changed over to peacetime production.

On the day of our wedding in March 1946 the London streets were slushy with melting snow turning to rain. The large Victorian church in Chelsea had survived bomb damage but it was dark and unrenovated with a host of neglected tombstones in the surrounding churchyard. Only a small number of people were there. Gerry was now working in the BBC but some of our friends had not yet been demobilised and were still wearing uniform. Aunts and uncles up from the country wore tweed coats and rainproof boots. Ma had a new tricorne hat for the occasion but Mark John's long black overcoat with the astrakhan collar looked a bit old-fashioned. It had been made for him in 1903 and was only ever used in the winters when he came back from Malaya on leave. Most of the years it had been kept in a trunk at his tailor's.

My wedding outfit was a French blue coat, a borrowed dress and a cap made of velvet ribbons. I carried a bouquet of pink tulips and forget-me-nots.

It was the start of a long marriage. The years before had laid firm foundations.

All this was ahead of me when, three years earlier, the *Stratheden* had sailed down the Clyde on a May morning to dock at Gourock. Along the river banks columns of smoke poured from the chimneys of the shipyards working at maximum capacity for the country at war. But now and then I saw clumps of trees, their leaves softly green with the fresh beauty of a Scottish spring and bluebells spreading beneath them down to the water's edge.

At Gourock we waited in the long queue to disembark. Officials were examining documents and when it came to our turn there was a tiresome delay. My mother and sisters had no passports. Before, nobody had ever asked to see them since we came to Africa and there had been no inspection when we went on board the *Stratheden*. It took hours, Ma explaining about the *Orcades* and authority conferring, while we hung about waiting to leave the ship like the rest of the passengers. Late in the afternoon we were able to get on the long boat train waiting in the station to take us south. It pulled out almost immediately afterwards.

Speeding through Britain all night, we had little sleep, sitting upright in a crowded carriage, blackout blinds drawn down and only a dim light in the ceiling. We were hungry too, as there had been no time to buy a sandwich since breakfast at Gourock.

When dawn came the train was passing through the environs of London. Names of stations had been removed from the platforms (to confuse the enemy if they invaded) but we knew that Clapham Junction was our next stop and where we would reach our journey's end.

I went into the corridor for my first sight of the city that had filled my thoughts so often since I left it.

It was going to be a warm day. The sun was shining on the south London streets, throwing long shadows on the slate roofs and blackened brick of the houses. In the gardens along the railway line lilac trees were in bloom. As the train slowed its pace I could see that many of these gardens were entirely vegetable plots, planted out in neat rows to ease the food shortages. Grass mounds, I guessed, had Anderson shelters underneath them. Inside families had sat for many a night listening to the crumps of falling bombs and the sound of ack ack fire, waiting for the All Clear. Few of the derelict houses had glass in the windows; in others criss cross tapes over the panes had preserved them during air raids.

Where bombs had fallen there were heaps of rubble. Sometimes one or two walls were still standing, and I glimpsed flowered wallpaper streaked with rain and soot. Once I caught sight of a mantelpiece up-ended and protruding from the debris of bricks and beams, and I imagined people sitting round the fireside before the bomb fell and their lives stopped forever. Weeds were growing in these places, softening the gaps in the rows with a thin green covering, and where the rose bay willow herb would soon flower for a second summer.

Nothing could cloud my happiness then as the train came slowly to a halt.

Passengers spilt out on to the platform and went to collect their luggage from the guards van at the end of the train. It was a long walk for us from the first carriage and we were hardly more than halfway along when, to our consternation, the train moved off again carrying our OK Bazaar suitcases with it. With dismay we watched it disappearing – to where we did not know.

Once again, it seemed, we were arriving at a new destination without any possessions. Fortunately they were retrieved the next day from Camberley.

People hurried past us, struggling with their bags or looking for one of the few elderly porters. A crowd of relatives and friends were waiting at the barrier to greet them.

Ahead of me my mother was walking rather wearily along the platform, one shoulder weighed down slightly by her bulging handbag. Her old black coat was creased and dusty from the train.

I caught her up and took her arm.

Postscript

I have come to the end of this tunnel. Outside the light is clear but there is little warmth in the winter sunshine.

The candle has burnt out. The charred wick lies in a mess of melting wax.